Understanding George Orwell's Animal Farm

A Complete GCSE Study Guide for Summe
AQA, WJEC and OCR Students

By Gavin Smithers

Another one of **Gavin's Guides** – study books packed with insight.
They aim to help you raise your grade!

Understanding George Orwell's Animal Farm is a complete study
guide and has been written both for students and teachers who are
preparing for GCSE in Summer 2016 and for those who face the exam
changes for Summer 2017.

Series Editor: Gill Chilton

The complete text of Animal Farm (Penguin) is widely available, including on Amazon. You will need a copy of this text, in paperback or as an e-book, to use alongside this Study Guide.

Let's get started

George Orwell's "Animal Farm" has been a favourite GCSE text for many years. It's easy to see why; it asks questions about tyranny and repression, about hope and fear, and about how the best of intentions can turn sour in the face of human selfishness and greed. It is a novel which is it almost impossible to read without being left with an impression. Its conclusion (at least on one level – we shall delve deeper to get on to other levels later) is satisfying.

It is also a short novel, with a moderate cast of "characters" who are mostly animal. Thus – whatever else you are studying for GCSE – this one will stand out.

However, to get a good grade at GCSE you will have to show understanding with some depth and be able to sustain your argument in an essay. This is where this study guide comes in.

If you've bought this guide because "Animal Farm" is a GCSE set text for you, then, in my opinion, you've just taken another step towards doing well in your exam.

Orwell asks us this; does the question "what is it like to live under a violent totalitarian dictatorship" matter? He says, yes, it does; because these regimes exist in different parts of the world, today, as they always have in the past. If we object to their repressive and cruel tactics, and we want to minimise the potential for such systems of government to control large parts of the world's population, we need to understand what enables them to exist in the first place, and what allows them to maintain their power.

If we can spot the early signs of totalitarian dictatorship- like detecting cancer- we should be able to treat it without major surgery. If we do not, we may not be able to treat it at all, and it may well kill us.

The rebellion on Animal Farm starts with a promise that the animals will have a fairer future and a better life, but their failure to make their leaders accountable soon turns democracy into dictatorship.

When those in charge use propaganda and intimidation to reinforce their power, the noble, original dream becomes a nightmare. For Orwell, freedom of speech is as crucial as freedom of thought, and the habitual revision of history by those in authority is immoral, dangerous, and easy to underestimate. The struggle to stand up for the ideals of a fair society, when the pigs are breaking and rewriting the commandments of Animalism, fails, because of the greed of the governing class and the passivity of the governed. The "fairy tale" is really a warning- a cautionary tale.

The lasting appeal of "Animal Farm" lies in its success in combining story-telling with political thinking- a difficult task!

The animal characters are simple, but engaging and individual. The allegory Orwell creates means that, as well as being characters in a story, they have a greater significance- a symbolic value. Napoleon is not just a dictatorial pig on a farm- he is a composite representation of the Emperor Napoleon 1st, Stalin, and other egomaniac and paranoid tyrants in all periods of history. Orwell's point is that, while the personnel may change, the question of who should govern us, and what powers they should have over us, is relevant to every citizen of every country in every generation.

Whichever exam board you are entered with, you will have to answer one question on the novel. You will have 45 minutes for this, and it will be worth about one sixth of the total marks available to you across the whole English Literature GCSE qualification.

The AQA board currently permits you to take a clean copy of the book into the exam; this will not be allowed from summer 2017 onwards, so you will need to know your way around the plot and have your references to the text secure in your own mind.

Summer 2016 Candidates

The OCR exam at present allows you 45 minutes to answer one question from a choice of two. You analyse a set extract, or you write an essay on the whole story, typically based on a theme (e.g. cruelty) or character (e.g. Snowball, or Pilkington and Frederick).

The examiners' reports note that there is a strong preference for the extract question, but that, where candidates do not focus on the wording of that question closely enough, answers lose marks. They say that the whole-book essay question is designed to give stronger candidates the chance to score a really good mark.

They want to see a clear personal response from you, with a close focus on language; they do not welcome too much history of the Soviet Republic, because you are sitting a literature exam, not a history one; so they are looking for you to demonstrate your understanding of Orwell's purpose and his writing technique.

Summer 2017 Candidates

In summer 2017, the question will change. Instead of being worth 15% of the total marks, this question will attract 25%, but it will be extended to 75 minutes.

Part A will be an extract question (45 minutes) which will ask you to compare a set extract with another extract from another (similar) text you have not seen before.

Part B requires you to write for 30 minutes on another moment or episode in "Animal Farm", to illustrate and analyse one of the main themes.

In this guide, I aim to give you a secure understanding of how Orwell writes, as well as the background context you need.

All examination boards are looking for the same elements in your answer-

1. Evidence that you are familiar with the plot and characters.

2. Proof that you can analyse your own feelings and responses as you read.

3. Ability to explain how Orwell manages (or manipulates!) our reactions.

This guide addresses all of those aspects of the novel, as well as the historical background. Understanding that context helps us to see very clearly what Orwell intends the meaning or message of his story to be.

Overall, about 75% of candidates will achieve grades A-C in English Literature GCSEs, with Bs and Cs the commonest grades.

My aim in writing this guide is to lead you towards the upper range of grades, by helping you to arrive at a thorough understanding of the novel, as well as giving you practical advice on how to manage your time in the exam and how to write a really effective exam essay.

So, why a Gavin's Guide?

You may have browsed online, or visited a bookshop, and found that there are several study guides on this text already. Many of them are useful for summarising the plot and the characters.

Few, if any, explain the context of the novella as thoroughly as this one, or concentrate so much on how Orwell manages and organises our response as we read. Understanding these aspects of the purpose of the novel- and showing your examiner that you do- will make it easier for you to achieve a higher grade.

What this short guide can do

This guide will help you to understand clearly what Orwell wanted to say when he wrote "Animal Farm"- and where that motivation came from. It will also help you to improve your essay technique.

For GCSE, it is not enough to know what happens in a novel. You need to be alert to the "why" and "how" of the way in which the writer has created the text. That includes being able to connect and relate events which take place several chapters apart; I highlight these connections for you.

So, to deepen your understanding, all you need is a few clear hours ….. and the willingness to begin with an open, curious mind.

This short interpretative guide is intended as a supplement to, not a substitute for, your lessons at school. To benefit most, you will need to have read the novella for yourself, all the way through, before you read the critical analysis you will find here.

Again, you may be interested in watching stage or film versions of the story. As with other GCSE texts, a stage version may be appearing in a theatre near you- check your local listings, and see whether a school trip is planned, or possible.

There is also a dramatized audio version available. This was aired on BBC Radio as a fully cast play and can be purchased on Amazon. But bear in mind that, on radio, or film or on stage, what you are hearing or watching is "based on" the book- it will be an adaptation, and a shorter, edited version of the original, with some action and some characters left out.

Later in this guide, I comment on the two commonly available film versions. Where directors of films and plays depart from the original written version, it is interesting to ask ourselves why. Multimedia versions of Orwell's story can heighten your awareness of the issue of artistic control, and how it shapes the novella, the play and the film versions in different ways. But…

Remember that your exam is not about other versions of the story; it's only about Orwell's original.

This is a literature exam, not a media studies one.

Watching film or stage versions will not, by itself, improve your essays or your understanding of Orwell's meaning. They might even confuse you, because they will obscure the careful structure Orwell built in his own telling of the tale. To understand what Orwell was doing, you need to read on……..

I am a private tutor in Broadway, Worcestershire and this book was initially written for my English Literature Students. In the same way that I help them achieve good grades, so I hope this will help you and so I also make the offer that you can email me at grnsmithers@hotmail.co.uk if you feel there is something you still don't understand- I'll hope to help you further.

This short, interpretative guide is intended as a supplement to, not a substitute for, teaching in a school.

It also comes with a big warning.

...this guide tells you what happens in the book, right from the start.

I make no apologies for 'plot spoiling' – as it is quite deliberate. A Study Guide is useful after you have read the novella – it is not a 'short-cut' that means you don't have to!

Only by looking at the structure of each scene and seeing how it breaks down (when you know in your head already how the book will 'turn out') can you gain full understanding.

So, by all means have a copy of the original text to hand, and a pencil and notebook as you read this Gavin's Guide – and let's get going together.

Politics and sensitive issues in 1945

There were a good many political issues at the time of this book's publication in 1945. They affected Orwell and his readers, so it is important you know about them too.

Orwell wrote "Animal Farm" between November 1943 and February 1944, but it was not published until August 1945 – after World War Two had ended - because publishers were sensitive about material which was negative towards the USSR, which this book is. They were sensitive about it because Stalin, and his country the USSR, had become a key ally of Britain and the USA.

Orwell was particularly proud of his achievement in creating Animal Farm because this was his first book which welded together a political and an artistic purpose.

The political purpose was to provide an allegorical critique of what he saw as the betrayal of the Russian Revolution in 1917 by Stalin- he described it as "a satirical tale against Stalin".

But Orwell also wanted to make a much broader point- to emphasise that popular revolutions can only make a lasting difference to the lives of the mass of working people when they remain "alert" to the abuse of power.

Orwell believed that what he wanted to say was so important that as many people as possible should be able to read and understand his thinking.

So he wrote Animal Farm with the conscious intention of producing a work which would be understood easily, and which would be easy to translate into foreign languages for an international readership.

Orwell felt that he had achieved a sense of symmetry in his narrative- we can see it in the contrast between the opening of the story and its end, the merging of all differences between pigs and humans, and the systematic, cynical dismantling and rewriting of the seven commandments. The idealistic dream at the start of the story contrasts with the nightmare of the pigs' control at the end, from which there is no escape.

Orwell ends his "fairy tale" with a pessimistic assessment that a necessary popular revolution can leave a nation in a worse position than the desperate one which prompted it in the first place.

At the end of chapter 10, the meeting of "pigs" (Communists and/or Fascists) with the human farmers (Britain/USA) refers to the four-day Tehran Conference in December 1943 between Churchill, Roosevelt and Stalin. Britain had been supporting the Soviets in their war with the Germans since 1941. The conference agreed a strategy to squeeze Hitler- the Western Allies would invade France, while the Russians would attack on the eastern front, aiming to divert German troops from France. The price for Stalin's support was the redrawing of national boundaries in Eastern Europe and a concession that Poland would become a Communist country, once Hitler was defeated.

Orwell could see that the future co-operation of Britain and the USA with Russia would be very uncomfortable; the Cold War would soon see the start of an uneasy stand-off between the communist East and the capitalist West, starting in 1947, and lasting until 1991.

Hitler's invasion of Russia in June 1941 was the largest military invasion in history. Millions of Soviet prisoners were starved to death, deliberately, as part of Hitler's plan to repopulate Eastern Europe with ethnic Germans. In 1939, Germany and Russia had undertaken not to fight each other, and agreed to divide Poland between them. They also had a trade pact which exchanged German armaments for Russian food and oil. The German invasion betrayed these agreements, and it surprised Stalin. It finally ground to a halt in the Battle of Moscow in December 1941; another attack on Russia in

1942 failed with the German defeat in the Battle of Stalingrad which ended in February 1943. That battle was possibly the decisive turning point in the whole of the Second World War.

The pro-Russian outlook in Britain in 1944 was understandable, but Orwell felt it was dishonest to ignore the way in which Stalinism terrorised and intimidated its own citizens, just because the Russian people had suffered barbaric ethnic cleansing at the hands of Hitler.

Several publishers rejected the book, raising objections about its overall point of view and its specifically and unsubtly anti-Soviet line. The artistic criticisms which came with the publishers' rejections may be masking a truer and more pragmatic judgment that this was no time to be ungrateful to a nation (Russia) which had suffered so much in its fight against Fascism, and done so much to help Britain.

Today, "Animal Farm" has a secure place in our literary heritage, because there has been plenty of time to evaluate the historical importance of Stalin, who died in 1953.

Orwell was right, in two important points he argued; that Russia, under Stalin, suppressed freedom of speech and freedom of thought, just as much as Fascism (which was worse than Communism, because it was deeply racist, too); and that Soviet propaganda should not be taken at face value by people in the West, who supposed that any ally of Britain's could not possibly oppress, slaughter and starve its own people. Orwell wasn't especially original or unique to think like this – all of us should know, from looking back at the course of history, that totalitarian dictatorships always behave like this. Stalin would be unlikely to be different from the rest.

George Orwell and his mission as a writer

Orwell was born in 1903 and he died in 1950. His real name was Eric Arthur Blair.

He is most famous for his novel "Nineteen Eighty-Four" (published in 1949) and his shorter novella or fable "Animal Farm" (published in London on 17 August 1945, and in the USA in August 1946). He wrote six novels in total, a great many essays, and several non-fiction books about his adventures among the poor in Paris and England, and as a soldier in the Spanish Civil War.

Orwell's personal values and drives are important to his writing. He went to a small private school in Eastbourne, then to Eton, and then into the Imperial Police in Burma. It was some years before he made a living from writing (from 1934 onwards), and even then his work as a print journalist took priority over writing novels.

His essays tell us a great deal about him. In particular, "The Prevention of Literature" (1946) sets out his deep-rooted hostility towards the way totalitarian states operate; "Why I write" (1946) explains his interests and methods; a long essay, "The English People" (1943), analyses our outlook as a nation, and the preface for the Ukrainian edition of "Animal Farm" in 1947 contains some valuable comments about what lies behind the writing of that story.

The issues of intellectual freedom, and of what Orwell called his "natural hatred of authority", lie at the heart of his writing. He argues that powerful people- the ruling politicians and thinkers, newspaper owners and broadcasters- can distort and rewrite history, obscure the truth and even pretend that inconvenient events never took place.

In "Animal Farm", Snowball masterminds, leads and wins the Battle of the Cowshed. Once his enemy Napoleon has exiled him, Napoleon's propaganda officer, Squealer, progressively downgrades and revises Snowball's role in it, until, finally, the animals accept (the complete lie) that Snowball actually led the attacking forces!

Although the other animals know, somehow, that they are being fed lies, the "official" version of events, backed up by the threat of violence against anyone who refuses to accept the propaganda, becomes accepted as the truth. In this way, powerful people can hide crimes against humanity which it suits them to keep hidden from public view and discussion.

Squealer also recites lists of statistics to "prove" to the animals that they have more food and better lives than in the old days- even when that is ludicrous, because they are constantly hungry and underfed.

Because their memories are poor, and because Squealer is accompanied by a pack of vicious killer dogs, the animals accept what he tells them, even when it is outrageously wrong.

Orwell described himself as a socialist out of "disgust" at how the poorest people in society live, rather than from some grand, abstract intellectual theory.

Similarly, what he saw and experienced as a journalist made him utterly opposed to the use of propaganda to mislead people. He believed that our need for Stalin's alliance in the war against Hitler led to the acceptance in democratic countries (England) of what he called "the Soviet myth"- a tendency to discount or ignore Stalin's false accusations and his genocidal purges of his political opponents.

He described Stalin as "barbaric and undemocratic", and he felt that he had a mission to show readers in Western Europe what had gone wrong in the USSR after 1930- "its transformation into a hierarchical society"- and how its original vision of socialism, which motivated the Russian Revolution in 1917, had become corrupted . He believed that people who live in democracies found it hard to understand how repressive the Nazi and the Soviet regimes really were, because the truth is hard to reach. The animals in his story allow Napoleon to kill some of their "comrades", in a very cruel and public way.

His purpose, in doing this, is simply to assert his power, and eliminate any opposition (like Stalin). Orwell shows us that the animals are wrong to accept this murderous violence, and weak. Their simple-mindedness is a key ingredient in Napoleon's unchecked evolution into a monstrous, immoral dictator. Orwell implies that, in allowing Stalin and his pigs to acquire total control, the Russian people have been equally feeble-minded; and that other peoples could easily make the same mistake.

A different sort of story…..

"Animal Farm" is a short tale, too short to be called a novel. Orwell himself subtitled it "A Fairy Story", but it has no fairies in it. Rather, it has a cast of farm animals, and it sees the world from their point of view. There is some humour in this- they see human beings as sly, lazy, selfish and devious. There is a tradition in literature of using animal fables to show us truths about being human- think of Aesop's "Fables", from which proverbs and sayings such as the Tortoise and the Hare, with its theme, 'slow and steady wins the race' are still with us, two and a half thousand years later; or "The Wind in the Willows", which has much to say about the nature of friendship and eccentricity.

Interestingly, we tend to associate animal stories with childhood. They lend themselves to presenting a simplified emotional world- animals are not evolved, so they have less complex thoughts and feelings than people.

This is vital to Orwell, because his animal characters have very little in the way of memory (they cannot remember what life was like before the Rebellion) and they find it impossible to find words to express their thoughts of unease, when the pigs repeatedly revise history to suit themselves.

One of Orwell's key themes is that the principles which prompt a revolution or shift in society can be forgotten, when the revolutionaries become established. Because his (intelligent) pigs are not challenged effectively by the other animals, the lack of intelligence among the horses, sheep, hens and other animals makes them passive, easily led and easily exploited.

Yet, if they only knew their own strength, pigs (in the story, mankind in real life) could not exploit them; Orwell believes that the rich classes exploit the working or labouring classes (the proletariat) in the same way men exploit animals' strength and capacity for work. He wrote the novella in 1943, but the ideas underpinning it had already been in his mind for the previous six years.

Orwell found it interesting that the English are happy to have the bulldog as a symbol of their national identity, because it is renowned as a stupid type of dog. He argues that the English tend to think of themselves as less intelligent than foreigners, and less logical, and that, as a nation, we are suspicious of those who have too much power and authority. We sympathise with the underdog; we do not accept that the end justifies the means, and we dislike bullying, terrorism and unfairness.

According to Orwell, the English are too relaxed about the need for a wide range of opinions, and too tolerant, for a communist revolution to be likely here.

One of the reasons why this story is so short- about a third as long as most novels- is that, by choosing farm animals as his characters, Orwell excludes the scope for character development and subtle characterisation which we associate with the full-length novel.

He makes this choice because his interests lie elsewhere- in concentrating on communicating his ideas about the dangers of dictatorships to a readership around the world.

George Orwell's reputation was as a political journalist and writer. By April 1944- after he had written "Animal Farm", but before the publication of "1984" (in 1949)- he had become even more concerned that totalitarian powers try to control their citizens' thoughts, as well as their words.

While England always tolerates a variety of views, and allows freedom of expression, those who control the newspapers and the broadcast word (remember that Orwell, by his own admission, hated authority figures) have a degree of influence over us which we are unconscious of and too unconcerned about. The media- like the politicians who have executive power- can change public opinion, and the values and outlook of a nation, by rewriting history, which is never recorded accurately and objectively.

It seems safe to assume that if Orwell were alive today he would approve of the growth in social media, because it is so much more democratic and impossible to control, in comparison with national newspapers, television and radio. He would have liked the idea that the truth would be told, if not by official news channels, then by witnesses to events, with their camera phones.

How to read Orwell's story

When you read "Animal Farm" for the first time, read it purely as a story; forget the allegorical dimension and the symbolic meanings. You will find that it works perfectly well as a narrative; the animals think they have achieved a fair society, without human beings to oppress them, but the pigs, especially Napoleon, progressively adopt human vices- they try to become more and more like humans- and the hard-working animals sense that they are no better off than they were before.

Memorably, at the very end of the story, the working farm animals are looking into the farmhouse from the outside, and the pigs are indistinguishable from humans.

As you read the fable, simply as a story, you will notice details which strike you as odd, or in need of explanation; why do so many animals confess to "crimes", for which they are killed, viciously, publicly and instantly, in chapter 7? Why is there so much about Snowball's alleged sabotage after he leaves the farm? Why are the neighbouring farms important? Why is a vet not brought on to the farm to treat Boxer in chapter 9?

The answer to these frequent puzzles is that there is another layer of meaning to the narrative; it is an allegory. **Allegory** is a very old literary form, or technique, but one which we rarely encounter nowadays. It works *by taking a truth about the world we live in- often a truth which it is difficult to discuss openly- and putting it into the fancy dress of a story.*

We still recognise the issue which is being investigated- we recognise the person in the fancy dress costume- but the disguise makes the issue under discussion less controversial, less personal, less heated, than it would be without its fancy dress.

Orwell wanted to write a veiled critique of what had happened in Russia since the Revolution of 1917, because he disapproved of the repressive and authoritarian dictatorship Stalin had managed to establish. In that sense, Animal Farm is Russia, and Napoleon is Stalin.

But Napoleon (the pig) has the name of another, earlier, revolutionary dictator- Napoleon Bonaparte of France. From this, we can infer that Orwell is interested not just in the autocratic excesses of Stalin, and the perverted outcome of the Russian Revolution, but, more widely, in the outcomes of other revolutions in other countries in other periods of history too.

While Napoleon is Stalin, he is more than that. He symbolises all dictators in all eras, not just Stalin in Russia.

How can we be sure that this allegory-building involves taking a character and making their identity more complex? Let's look at two other examples.

Moses the black raven is introduced to us in chapter 2, where he is clearly a symbol for the "mad monk" Rasputin. Rasputin was a priest who helped the Russian Royals during the Russian Revolution of the early 20th century, but was assassinated in 1916.

Moses the raven reappears in chapter 9, after being absent for several years; again, he represents to the other animals the escapist promise or vision of a better life after death.

Orwell's point here is that, even to an atheist totalitarian regime, the Church has its uses. The comfort it offers to the oppressed and suffering makes them less likely to launch a counter-revolution. Moses the raven therefore exists in the story to link the Joneses in chapter 2 with Russia, and the misery and suffering of its people over a sustained period.

In the same way, in the story of Animal Farm, Frederick, who owns one of the neighbouring farms (countries), and who is "feared and hated" by the Russians in chapter 8, is a symbol of Adolf Hitler.

The negotiations over the sale of the pile of timber, then, allude to the non-aggression pact Stalin made with Germany in 1939, and the heavily armed attack Frederick leads on Animal Farm represents Hitler's invasion of Russia in 1941. By extension, the farmer Pilkington becomes Churchill (or a composite of Great Britain and the USA), and the acrimonious party in chapter 10 represents the strategic conference in Tehran in November 1943, where Stalin and Churchill clashed over their intentions for the post-war map of Europe, and of Poland in particular. It is significant that Frederick/ Hitler is missing from the delegation of farmers in that chapter, after his attack on the windmill (which could be seen to represent Hitler's attack on Moscow).

But "Frederick" is also a more general name for a succession of real, historical kings of Germany, Prussia, Denmark and Norway. Orwell may be thinking not just of Hitler here, but also of King Frederick William 1 of Prussia (1688-1740), another despot and an aggressive militarist from an earlier era of German history.

Why does Orwell take such care to make his characters into these composite and multi-faceted figures? There are two explanations. The first is the "fancy dress" one. At a time when Russia was a key ally of Britain in the war against Hitler, being too personally critical of Stalin was politically sensitive. This is why several publishers refused to be responsible for distributing "Animal Farm".

But, in my view, the second explanation is much more important.

It is this; Orwell's leading emphasis is on the Stalinist regime, but *he is interested in the character and consequences of revolution generally*. And he is particularly concerned *about the relationship between the governed and those who govern them*, not just from a Marxist perspective, but also from an English one, via the reference Old Major makes to the 17th century English philosopher Thomas Hobbes – you'll read more about Hobbes' views later on in this study guide.

Detailed commentary

Chapter 1

The story begins with a number of farm animals filing into the large barn at the Manor Farm; three dogs, the pigs, the hens and pigeons, sheep and cows; two cart-horses, a white goat, and a donkey; some motherless ducklings; Mollie the white mare; and a cat. The raven stays away because the ideology of the meeting is not religious. Old Major the pig's dream of a rebellion threatens to supplant the dream of animal heaven- called Sugarcandy Mountain- which the raven uses as his special knowledge, and his excuse for being fed on the farm without doing any work.

Some of the animals are given names- the dogs are Bluebell, Jessie and Pincher; the cart-horses are Boxer and Clover; the goat is Muriel, the donkey Benjamin, "the foolish, pretty white mare" is Mollie, and the raven is Moses. The other animals do not have names, because their significance is only as a group, not as individuals. The hens, for example, become a symbol for the kulaks- Russian peasant farmers who were to be impoverished under Stalin's plans to reorganise agricultural production, and who were treated ruthlessly when they tried to protect their own property from state ownership.

The fact that there is a dream (or an alleged dream) should alert us to the fact that we are dealing with an allegory here.

In literature, a dream vision is a literary device for revealing what the dreamer thinks is a truth, and which we cannot grasp in our normal state of being awake; or, as in the case of this dream of Old Major's, a dream may be regarded as a revelation of imaginative possibilities which we cannot reach otherwise.

There is a long tradition of visionary dreaming, in Old and Medieval English literature. We are used, too, to visionary speeches, such as

Martin Luther King's "I have a dream" speech of 1963, which set out a vision of a post-racist society in which it is accepted that "all men are created equal".

"Allegory" is originally a Greek term, meaning "veiled language"- that is, something which hints at or alludes to something else. In literary practice, this means a story behind the obvious story. We now have a term to describe the process of detecting the metaphorical or figurative meaning of such a text- "allegoresis"- the act, and the art, of reading a story as an allegory.

While it is generally understood that Orwell revisits and represents aspects of the Russian Revolution in his tale, the allegory goes wider than this. It is both specific in its focus on real historical events in Russia and Europe, and more abstract, in its questioning or analysis of social and political theory.

The pig Old Major says that **"our lives are miserable, laborious and short"**, and his speech emphasises- indeed, dramatizes- the violent methods by which pigs, horses and dogs are put to death by human beings.

Both of these elements point us, not just towards Karl Marx, but to the English philosopher Thomas Hobbes (1588-1679). He wrote that, in the absence of a proper monarchy (or government by one person), the state of nature will be chaotic and violent.

He calls this a "summum malum"- the greatest evil- in which people will not work, or cultivate the land, or build anything, because their lives will be dominated by "continual fear and danger of violent death, and the life of man (is) solitary, **poor, nasty, brutish and short**". It is ironic that this is precisely the type of life the animals come to experience under Napoleon's dictatorship.

It is intriguing that Hobbes' phrase matches Old Major's so closely; **miserable** and **poor** or **nasty** are interchangeable; both use the word

short; and **laborious** is a suitable substitute for **brutish**, considering that Old Major does not wish to undermine the human qualities of the animals by calling them brutes.

The setting of the novella- a farm in rural England- and the animals' anthem, "Beasts of England"- confirm, further, that Orwell's interests lie in the broader international area of Western Europe, as well as in recent events in Russia. On Animal Farm, pigeons spread news and rumours, flying from one farm to another; Orwell is interested in how we can be misinformed about what is really going on in other nations (or on other farms).

In its broadest sense, Marxism categorises society as consisting of the proletariat (people who work) and the bourgeoisie (the people who own assets, and take for themselves the profits generated by the work of the proletariat). Marxism predicts that, as the unfairness of the inequality between these two groups becomes clear to the proletariat, there will be a social revolution, which will do away with the bourgeoisie and replace it with cooperative ownership (of land, machinery etc).

This post-revolution condition is a society which practises socialism. Marx anticipated that the equalising influence and instincts of socialism would then mature into communism- a humane society where everyone is treated according to their needs, and the weak and needy are supported by society as a whole. Farming, for example, then becomes a process of producing the food its occupants need for their own (and other people's) use, but without the motive of making a profit- which, Marx believes, leads to the oppression and exploitation of workers, or, in this case, farm animals. The theory of Marxism is that, by getting rid of the private ownership of assets, you end imbalances of power and the need for revolution, which can be violent.

Marx said that the claim that "the interests of the capitalist and those of the worker are…one and the same" is a lie, and that exploitation is the gap between what a worker produces and what they receive for it.

He argues, therefore, that if the means of production are owned in common, exploitation should not exist.

Old Major echoes this exactly. He argues that Man's claim to protect the animals on the farm is false- Man exploits them, works them almost to death, virtually starves them, and slaughters them when they are no longer useful.

Hobbes' contrasting view is that someone must have the authority to govern in every society. The main, and most important, responsibility of that person is to protect the people he governs from physical harm; the governed give up some of their rights as individuals, in exchange for safety; this is a "social contract". In particular, strong and effective government will protect the citizen from the risk of violent death, or the slaughter Old Major speaks of. The "sovereign" has the right to censor "opinions and doctrines", because he must do "whatever he thinks necessary" to preserve peace and security.

Napoleon is a dictator (or tyrant), but, on Hobbes' view, he is entitled to use his complete or absolute power- given to him by the consent of the other animals- to behave like a monarch, and pursue their security. Squealer claims that this has been done, when there is no need to regard the Rebellion as ongoing (chapter 7)- no external or internal enemy remains. Ironically, Napoleon is a corrupt dictator; the only person whose safety he works for is his own (and his own children's).

Hobbes would say that, when the "sovereign" ceases to protect the ordinary citizen, he loses his right to the allegiance of the population as a whole, and his authority (as King Charles 1 had, arguably, done, when he was executed in 1649, and when Oliver Cromwell replaced him).

The problem with Marxism (as with Old Major's speech) is that it concentrates on the *vision* of equality, without addressing Hobbes's intuition that societies always need a governing "sovereign". Orwell shows us Napoleon beginning to use censorship and his own repressive authority to stamp out dissent; not to secure peace, but to secure his own position, privileges and power (such as his private army of dogs, his school for his own children, and his personal supply of beer and whisky).

Critical comment on "Animal Farm" tends to concentrate exclusively on the parallel with Russia and Stalin. But we need to pay attention to the fact that Old Major talks about both the Marxist vision and the Hobbesian model of government which we are familiar with, in capitalist countries. Someone has to be in charge; Napoleon, being a pig, is greedy, lazy and calculating, and he turns out to be a fatally bad choice.

Old Major's rhetoric persuades the animals, and it leads to the code of Animalism and the seven commandments. But the rest of the story shows us how the pigs then progressively break and redefine the commandments, without any effective challenge from the governed. The combination of propaganda, intimidation, and the animals' stupidity allows Stalin/Napoleon to remain all-powerful, even though he is not delivering the peace for his citizens which Hobbes says is the basis of the social contract.

Old Major's speech is key to the tale, because it sets out the criteria on which the success or failure of the Rebellion are to be judged. Can a (Russian) Revolution turn Marx's vision into a lasting reality? Or is Hobbes right- will there have to be a governing class or individual, and, if so, how can they remain "equal", and what does their right to govern depend on? Orwell would say that the successful government of any nation depends on the willing consent of its citizens, and he draws our attention to the sad truth that the animals' lack of intelligence and linguistic capability means that, even when their consent is unwilling, they lack the capacity to overturn a tyrant. At the end of his story, Orwell's animals are condemned to live under a cruel pig regime for the future, as well as now, because Napoleon has trained his children to continue to enforce the power of the pig, when he himself is dead.

Old Major's speech in chapter one is important. It is the base point from where we can measure what happens (that is so wildly different). It sets out the aims and ambitions of the Rebellion. As we read the story, we find ourselves comparing later events with the mood and motivation of this speech.

He addresses the animals as "comrades".

Our lives, he says, are **miserable, laborious and short**- a life of being forced to work, being fed the minimum, and, when no longer useful, "slaughtered with hideous cruelty". Animals in England are not free; their lives are just day after day of unremitting misery and slavery.

The farm- and all farms in England- could support a much better way of life; the problem is that human beings steal "nearly the whole of the produce of our labour". It is the tyranny of Man which makes the animals hungry, overworked and miserable. Man "consumes without producing". It follows that, if there were no enslavement to humans, the animals would keep "the produce of our labour", and be "rich and free".

He argues that it is wrong that the milk the cows produce is drunk by humans, and that the eggs are sold instead of hatched. Clover's foals were sold, and will not be there to comfort her in her old age. The inference is that the animals would have a domestic/family life of a different quality, without the tyranny of human owners (hens and cows are herd or pack animals, but it suits Orwell to give them the social instincts of humans, and he amuses us in doing this).

Then he raises the point that no farm animal dies a natural death; they all face "the cruel knife in the end". Pigs will be slaughtered before the age of one. Jones drowns his dogs when they can no longer work; Boxer will be sent to the knacker's yard for slaughter (this does indeed happen, in chapter 9, but with a cruel irony this is on the instructions of the pig, Napoleon, not Jones the farmer!).

Major's speech is rhetorical, and it uses graphic language to drive home the brutality of an animal's life (**slaughtered**, **hideous cruelty**, **scream your lives out**, **cut your throat**, **boil you down**).

See what rhetorical devices you can find (hint – look out for: the rule of three; repetition; contrasts; pathos; rhetorical questions; variety in sentences lengths and structures; direct address; exclamations; imperatives; the balancing of reasoned argument and emotive language).

His call to action is an exhortation that the animals must work towards a rebellion, although he does not know when that will come about; he suspects that it will be not in their own lifetimes- perhaps Major says this because the life of most of the farm animals is so short. It also of course serves to make it a more dramatic read for us when it happens almost right away!

Napoleon says that men lie when they say that they and animals each promote a better life for the other; they are driven, truly, only by self-interest. Therefore, "all men are enemies" and "all animals are comrades". Animals have a "duty of enmity towards Man".

He warns that, once the rebellion has succeeded, animals must not "adopt his vices". He lists seven of these, plus the rule that animals must never kill another animal, and the principle that "all animals are equal".

Five of these points become some of "the seven commandments" (in chapter 2) - no animal shall wear clothes, sleep in a bed, drink alcohol, or kill another animal; plus the equality rule. The other four- that animals must not live in a house, smoke tobacco, touch money, or engage in trade- do not.

<u>Ironically, of course, none of these instructions is still in force by the end of the fable.</u>

Major's overriding warning- that "no animal must ever tyrannise over his own kind"- is ignored, in that Napoleon seizes power by force in chapter 5, and becomes a farmer himself by the end of the fable.

Major says that he "cannot describe" his dream, which was of the Earth after "man has vanished". Instead, the words of the lost/forgotten anthem "Beasts of England" returned in his dream. The song stirs the animals "into the wildest excitement"; they repeat the song five times.

His speech is not, in fact, about the dream- he cannot describe it- or about the passing on of "such wisdom as I have" about "the nature of this life of ours". He simply says that animals live a miserable life, of hunger, overwork and eventual slaughter, and that they should cultivate hatred and enmity, and rebel, so that they can be "rich and free" by keeping what they produce.

The vision here is of a socialist utopia, where everyone is equal, and no-one oppresses or tyrannises "his own kind".

The appeal is that, somehow, having land in common ownership will magically reduce the workload needed to cultivate it (it will not); and that malnourishment will be a thing of the past, because there will be no humans siphoning off what is produced (this is potentially true).

The idea that animals desire a family life akin to that of humans is fanciful; so, too, is the assertion that animals only kill each other because of human tyranny. In fact, predatory animals kill other animals as a matter of Nature. Major complains that Man is "lord of all the animals", although he has no superior skills- he cannot lay eggs or catch rabbits.

Major appears to be a "wise and benevolent" elder statesman. Why has it taken him twelve years to formulate his philosophy of revolution? Is his argument justified, or is it really the politics of envy?

His argument is simplistic, in skating over- by simply denying- the possibility that Man and animals really do achieve more, together, than they could independently; and in dismissing the idea that animal welfare must be of some concern to Man, because the animals are useful to him.

The anthropomorphism- the giving to animals the qualities of people- is amusing, but also quietly unsettling. We tend to think of animals as lacking emotional breadth and depth, because they are unevolved. But these animals can anticipate their own deaths, and how those deaths will be administered; they can remember the wrongs done to them in the past; they have a sense of family and of morality. They are not intellectually especially bright, but they respond to emotive appeals and they seem ready to be led.

Chapter 2

We are not told which year the story is set in; but Old Major dies three nights later, and this chapter takes us from then (early March) forwards three months.

The pigs are the cleverest animals on the farm, and, from that group, a trio of pigs emerges- Napoleon, Snowball and Squealer.

Note how they are described.

Napoleon is a practical, decisive user of power, used to "getting his own way". Snowball is more lively and imaginative. Squealer is a persuasive speaker, who can "turn black into white". He is a propagandist. If Napoleon is Stalin, then Snowball is Trotsky and Squealer is Lenin (both Russian revolutionaries in the 1920s). Squealer becomes a propagandist later- like Hitler's aide, Goebbels, he is the mouthpiece for a regime of pigs which believes itself racially superior; and, as the story develops, Napoleon also behaves like Napoleon Bonaparte, in seizing power for himself.

Before the Revolution, these three pigs have turned what Old Major (Marx) had to say into "Animalism", which is a "complete system of thought". It starts with the concept of a proletarian revolution, based on the belief that a class war is inevitable. For Orwell, dramatizing this as a rebellion of animals against humans is neat, and almost bloodless.

We know that Mr Jones represents the Tsar (the hereditary ruler of Russia), Nicholas 2nd, because he is accompanied by Moses, the raven, who is a representation of the "mad monk" Rasputin. The description of the interior of the farmhouse, with its print of Queen Victoria (another European monarch), turns it into a smaller-scale model of the Winter Palace, in St Petersburg; this means that Animal Farm is, metaphorically, Russia.

When Orwell finished his tale, in February 1944, of the three original leaders of the Russian Revolution only Stalin was alive (he continued to be, effectively, the sole ruler of the USSR until his death in 1953). Lenin had died in 1924, and Trotsky was assassinated (in exile, in Mexico) in 1940, on Stalin's orders.

Instead of using vaguely Russian names for his key characters, Orwell adopts English ones, as well as the name "Napoleon", *not because he hopes that the references to Stalin will thus be less direct, but because he wants to widen the scope of his discussion of the nature of dictatorship.*

There are farms in most countries, and in England; <u>is it possible, he is asking us, that such a rebellion could take place here?</u> His own view was that there would not be a revolutionary uprising in Britain because we are not much good at civil war; we would rather listen to, and tolerate, a wide range of opposing views than kill others for having opinions we ourselves disagree with. We are not temperamentally easily led by people who have an ideology based on the opposition of "good" and "evil".

Napoleon 1 (1769-1821) was Emperor of France from 1804-1815. He had grown up at the time of the French Revolution (a series of events between 1789 and 1799), which, like the Russian Revolution, deposed its monarchy and replaced it with another type of government. Both Napoleon and Stalin saw themselves as social reformers and benign dictators; they both modernised their countries, at a time where feudalism and the economic dominance of old methods of farming were coming to an end, with profound social consequences.

However, in the light of history, both men can be judged as tyrannical, and extremely ruthless in their exercise of power. Both became paranoid; a cult of personality grew up around both of them.

Both, significantly, recognised the power of propaganda, and they used it to create a public perception of themselves which would inspire confidence and awe (and fear) in their own nation, and help them to stay in power.

After Napoleon's defeat at the Battle of Waterloo in 1815, the French monarchy was restored, just as the English one had been in 1660 (Charles 2nd). Napoleon was the most familiar European despot/dictator before Hitler and Stalin. Orwell's choice to adopt his name for the main pig in "Animal Farm" widens the scope of the novel's examination of ways of governing, beyond the modern communist state in the USSR, to include the other types of government which Thomas Hobbes analysed. Remember that Hobbes was writing at the time when the English republic (albeit still headed by one man, Oliver Cromwell) replaced the monarchy between 1649 and 1660.

Chapter 2 shows us that revolutions start with arguments and theories; revolutionary discussion begins to motivate the (normally peaceful and passive) worker to throw off his oppression, and to embrace violence as the means of doing that.

The aim of such a revolution is to correct the inequality between the producers of wealth (the workers or proletariat) and those who own the means of production (the "bourgeoisie"). After the revolution, assets are owned co-operatively, not privately, and the socialist economy then aims not to make a profit but to meet the needs of everyone in the population.

In taking old Major's ideas, and turning them into rules by which the animals must live and calling them "Animalism", Napoleon and Snowball resemble both the authors of Marxist Communism (Marx and Engels) and the political revolutionaries, the Bolsheviks, in Russia.

At first, the animals are both slow to understand the ideology of revolution, and apathetic about it. They fear that, without their farmer Jones, they will starve; and Moses the raven reminds them about Sugarcandy Mountain. His sermons about this invented place encourage the simplistic belief that we will be rewarded in heaven for being compliant, and obedient, or unrebellious, during our lifetime. This message serves to reinforce the status quo, and discourage revolution.

Marxist theory explains that the "base", or values, of a society conditions its ideology- it enables a ruling class and the authority of religion. Once the "base" starts to conflict with the "superstructure" of the established social hierarchy, the seeds of revolution are sown. The pigs, here, have to "argue very hard" to persuade the other animals to give up their belief in Heaven- supported by the cart-horses, Boxer and Clover, who are not bright enough to think for themselves.

Mollie is a white mare, and she sees particularly little benefit in a socialist rebellion; this positions her as the symbol of the "white" Russians, whom the Bolsheviks went on to defeat. The two paragraphs which describe the neglected state of the farm (Russia) and Jones' (Tsar Nicholas 2nd's) withdrawal reflect the condition of Russia in 1915 and 1916.

The rebellion in chapter 2 is a spontaneous uprising, on a Saturday, Midsummer's Eve; for us, this would be about 23 June. The flight of Mr Jones, followed by his wife and Moses the raven, corresponds to the February Revolution in Russia in 1917, after which the Tsar resigned. The second (October) revolution that year was organised by Lenin and Trotsky, and it put the Bolsheviks in charge of what would now be a socialist state.

The animals celebrate the flight of their human oppressors by burning the chains and knives and restraining equipment which symbolised and emphasised the nature of their slavery.

The next morning, Snowball and Napoleon break down the farmhouse door; the animals make an awestruck tour of the luxurious interior, which is reminiscent of the Tsar's Winter Palace.

While Snowball adopts a suitably revolutionary approach, as the era of Animalism begins- saying that no animal must wear clothes, or hats, or ribbons, because they are the "mark of a human being"- Mollie is still susceptible to the charm of such accessories, and the other animals tell her off.

They feel comfortable about owning the land, but they refuse to make use of the farmhouse- the habitat of humans- and resolve to keep it as a museum. This is one of the many decisions which become ironic once the pigs start to acquire the human taste for power, luxury and home comforts.

Symbolically, Snowball repaints the name of the farm on the gate (Animal Farm instead of Manor Farm), and he and Napoleon introduce the seven commandments of Animalism, an "unalterable Law" under which the animals will operate "for ever after". Snowball is enthusiastic and altruistic, but Napoleon is selfish and scheming. Very soon, he will start to rewrite the "unalterable Law" to suit himself.

Painting the commandments on the end wall of the barn is intended as a visual reminder. For the animals, difficulties arise because they cannot read the writing accurately. Napoleon and Squealer will exploit this lack of literacy, when they change and weaken the commandments, rewriting the ideals and diluting the moral force of the rebellion in order to maintain Napoleon's power and control.

In their ideological zeal to prove themselves better at harvesting than the human farmers, the pigs forget to milk the cows. When the cows are milked, and have produced five buckets of milk, the animals hope that, just as before the rebellion, it will be added to their feed; but Napoleon makes no such promise, and keeps the milk himself.

It is shocking that, so soon after the revolution, he should start to exploit the animals, and fail to give them back what they have produced- because that principle, of sharing the produce, is at the very heart of the Marxist/socialist theory which had persuaded the animals of the need for revolution in the first place.

The commandments are a little like Moses' ten commandments in the Old Testament (which were written down, on tablets of stone- we use the phrase "tablet of stone" to mean something which cannot be changed)- they are what makes the society of the animals better than the cruel, selfish society of human farmers.

They are taken directly from Old Major's speech in Chapter 1, just before he relates his "dream".

They concentrate on behavioural and social rules- there is to be no murder. The ban on wearing clothes, or sleeping in a (comfortable) bed, or on drinking alcohol, has the air of a monastery or a religious cult. The commandments label animals and birds as friends, and anything on two legs as enemies; the distinction is not watertight, and leaves practical loopholes.

The first one, about where that leaves birds, is easily overcome. There is a robust discussion on how birds, because they have wings that propel for motion rather than hands that only work, are covered under the 'four legs good' category.

But the idea that "all animals are equal" turns out not to be sustained- Orwell wants to make the point that, as soon as someone becomes more powerful than the rest, and makes decisions, they will assume higher status and will then tend to want privileges for themselves, making the concept of equality rhetorical and hollow.

The commandments are cleverly done, because they embody idealistic aims, and we feel that they reflect the animals' essential goodness, simplicity, and lack of education. There is no indication of how breaking the commandments will be dealt with. This is naïve, as it leaves a power vacuum which Napoleon will step straight into. Once he has taken control, he will never let go, because he is too clever to be accountable to the other animals.

Chapter 3

The animals are content at first with the benefits of the rebellion, but the narrative points out that they are not by any means equal, in practice, because of the differences among and between them in literacy and intelligence. The pigs are the cleverest animals, so they take on an executive or management role, supervising the manual work, but doing none of it themselves. They subtly address the other animals as "comrades"- pretending they are treating them as equals, even as they are exploiting them.

The pigs then define themselves as the intelligentsia, the brains of the new society. With shocking hypocrisy, they say that, even though they may not even like milk and apples, those items must be reserved for them alone, to maintain their health and well-being. This breaks the rule that all animals are equal, because it treats the working animals as inferior; but the sheep, horses and hens are not bright enough to challenge the basis of the idea.

Later on, Boxer becomes ill (and dies) because he is overworked. His strength, loyalty and dedication to hard manual work are taken for granted. The description of Boxer, and his personal motto ("I will work harder!"), reflect the socialist belief in the dignity of hard work. Like most of the animals, he sees himself as a worker, not a thinker. In doing so, he allows the pigs to set themselves up as superior beings, and this allows the first cracks in the construct of equality to appear.

The sense of common ownership and common purpose means that, with this fresh start, there is no stealing and no arguing on the farm. Mollie's frequent absences from work, and the cat's, are overlooked because, in a socialist society, everyone works "according to his capacity" and everyone's needs are met from what has been produced by the communal effort.

Orwell is good at conveying, here, the sense of fulfilment and satisfaction we feel when we are part of a group working for a shared aim. The animals take comfort from this feeling throughout the story, when they are suffering the most. That makes it harder for them to develop any sense that they need to rebel again, however badly Napoleon treats them.

Benjamin, the donkey, always takes a long view- he believes that nothing much changes, whoever is in charge, or however society is organised.

His world-weary cynicism throughout the tale chimes with Orwell's own views that, however passionate your ideology, in the end, revolutions fail, and the underlying issue of inequality and poverty remains very difficult to solve.

Rather like the instruction in the Old Testament's ten commandments, although it is not included in the seven commandments, the animals do not work on Sundays (yet). Their belief in Sugarcandy Mountain has gone; instead of any religious feeling or practices, there is a secular ceremony now, where the green and white flag of the Rebellion is raised. It is made from a green tablecloth, with a white horn, and a hoof painted in white on it. The flag symbolises the green fields of England and the power over it of the animal rebellion. Orwell makes his flag a little like the Soviet flag, which has a hammer and sickle on a red background, in case we miss the point that it is a revolutionary symbol.

Because there is no religion to observe, the Sunday meetings become a forum for organising the work on the farm, with resolutions which are voted on (like a trade union meeting, or a committee meeting); but they become a sterile and fractious debating arena for Napoleon and Snowball, who always oppose each other's ideas, because they are involved in a struggle for personal power (remember Thomas Hobbes' belief that the best form of society is one where **one** man has complete power, by the consent of all citizens).

The resolutions only ever come from the pigs, who have taught themselves to read and write. The other animals are, at best, semi-literate (except for Benjamin the donkey). Their difficulty with reading and writing extends to a difficulty thinking clearly, too.

The meetings end with a ritual singing of the anthem of the revolution, "Beasts of England"- a way of reminding the animals of their common purpose and their shared ideology. Because the stupider animals cannot remember the seven commandments, the slogan "Four legs good, two legs bad" becomes a summary of them. This is an over-simplification, which gives the pigs too much room for manoeuvre. It also prepares the ground for the moment in chapter 10 when the pigs have learned to walk on their hind legs- a moment which combines comedy, irony and horror, because it dramatizes the pigs' elitism and their blatant, cynical abandoning of the principles of Animalism and equality.

Orwell stresses that the first harvest after the rebellion was good, and that the animals made a success of it, even though they were handicapped by a lack of animal-friendly (or modern) technology. With the "petit bourgeois" Mr Jones and his human parasites gone, there is more food and "more leisure" (though Orwell does not explain how this comes to be the case). He means us to see a parallel with life in Russia after the 1917 revolution. In the early days after a revolution, life can appear to be better than it had been before.

Snowball is busy setting up various committees, which aim to improve the education of the workers and enable them to be more productive, but this is contrary to Nature (the Wild Comrades' Re-education Committee tries to tame wild rabbits and rats, which is, by definition, impossible). Napoleon is not interested in using the revolution to improve the education or the minds of the adult animals. He has taken the nine puppies of Jessie and Bluebell, and is keeping them out of sight. Because they are forgotten about, and not integrated into the society on the farm, he can retain and train them as his vicious private army.

He is preparing, entirely selfishly, to become a dictator- by force, if he meets any resistance. He wants to be the head of a repressive, totalitarian state (just like Hitler, as well as Stalin), and, as we will discover before long, he has the cunning to achieve all of his self-serving ambitions, because he understands the power of violence.

The chapter ends on a note which we, reading it, feel uncomfortable with- the mystery of what has happened to the milk the cows produced at the end of chapter 2.

The pigs have consumed it themselves, without sharing it; and they will do the same with apples which fall from the trees, and the whole apple crop when it is ready. This is sheer (pig-like) greed- endorsed by both Napoleon and Snowball- and a clear breach of the principle that all animals are equal, and the principle that, in a socialist society, everyone shares equally in what is produced.

They send Squealer to rebut any accusation that they are being selfish, or seeking privileges for themselves; he claims that, if the pigs are not given all the brain food they need, "Jones would come back". We understand that this is untrue, or at least an over-simplification.

However, it is just the sort of oversimplification the working animals cannot see through. They are being taken advantage of by creatures with a slightly better intellect then theirs- which is precisely what had enslaved them to Mankind in the first place.

Orwell pointed to this as a crucial moment in the tale, with the decisive shift of power it brings; **if the animals had challenged the theft of the milk**, Napoleon would not have been able to plot and plan his way to complete authority and unchallenged power.

In failing to stand up to the dictator at this stage, the animals have already sealed their fate, and, as a result, they will go on to have new experiences of misery, oppression, slavery and deprivation, worse than anything they have experienced before.

Chapter 4

This short chapter relates the Battle of the Cowshed- the facts of which will be revised by Napoleon, later, to prove Orwell's point that totalitarian regimes rewrite history, whenever it suits them.

It also sets the scene beyond the farm boundaries, for the first time. Just as Napoleon is a composite "great dictator" figure, drawn from Stalin and Hitler as well as Napoleon Bonaparte, so the neighbouring farms are symbolic of countries, but cannot be interpreted absolutely strictly as any one individual country.

Mr Jones is in exile in the pub, plotting an attempt to recapture the farm. The other farms are Foxwood, which is poorly run by the old-fashioned Pilkington, who is more interested in hunting and fishing than in making his farm efficient and productive; and Pinchfield, which is "smaller and better kept" by its owner, the hard-headed Frederick.

Snowball and Napoleon send pigeons out every day to spread their tale of socialist rebellion, and take the theme of "Beasts of England" to an international audience. The farmers nearby are afraid of the potential for similar revolts by their own animals, so they spread negative stories about primitivism and starvation on Animal Farm (in the revolutionary socialist republic). They have to change their story when it becomes clear that the animals are not starving; they say, next, that such a rebellion is unnatural (an argument Tsar Nicholas 2nd had used).

The (western European) farmers' use of propaganda is much blunter and less skilful than Napoleon's will prove to be. Orwell says that the truth about life in a communist state was "distorted" because of the "vague" rumours said that it was a "wonderful farm". Here, he is alluding to what he called the myth about Russia under Stalin in the decade leading up to his writing "Animal Farm". Orwell felt that the propaganda coming out of Russia sanitised the brutality of life there, under Stalin. At the same time, he is making the point that anti-communist propaganda, based on an ideological aversion to communism, can be completely inaccurate, too.

Birds take up the tune of the anthem "Beasts of England"; animals on other farms become less co-operative and obedient towards humans; and so the men decide to launch a counter-revolution, to recapture the farm from the animals.

The attack comes on October 12th. Jones has a gun, and the men who come with him have sticks. Snowball sets a defensive trap; a co-ordinated attack by (dive-bombing) pigeons and other small species, a tactical retreat, and then an ambush by the horses and cows enables the attack to be routed in the space of five minutes. One sheep dies, which is less loss of life than in most battles. This makes it appear a comedy or cartoon skirmish. There is a neat little joke- Boxer says he has "no wish to take life, even human life", in a reversal of the chain of evolution, which puts human life at the top of the list, and animal life at the bottom.

Napoleon and his dogs are nowhere to be seen during the battle. Napoleon is in fact a coward, who cares only for his own safety. He does not lead by example, but by stealth. Even in the Battle of the Windmill, in chapter 8, where there is no Snowball, we find Napoleon "directing operations from the rear".

It is important that we remember- and, if necessary, refer back to- this very clear and factual account of the battle, because Squealer will alter history by telling the animals that their memories are unreliable, and that Snowball was not brave. Eventually, the outrageous lie- that Snowball was fighting for the other side- will become possible, and then it will become accepted, by the animals (but not by the reader), as the truth. The military decorations reflect the bravery of the animals who did the fighting- Snowball, Boxer, and the dead sheep. Even here, though, there is a distinction- the sheep is only given a "second class" decoration.

The equalities of animalism are being nibbled at, by the pigs, who had taught themselves to read and write. They are beginning to seek ways of turning their superior intelligence and skills into a form of elitism. If Animal Farm had a university, only pigs would be allowed to take degrees!

The last three paragraphs of the chapter make it clear that the historical parallel to the Battle of the Cowshed is the second revolution in Russia in 1917, which drove out the provisional government and established the Bolsheviks (Communists) as in control, and empowered to make their particular ideology the official system of government.

Cleverly, Orwell makes the allegorical meaning less specific by putting two historical references in the wrong order in this chapter. This is important because it reminds us that we are not reading a parody of a particular era in history, but an allegory about how people tend to feel and behave the world over. The first reference is to the unease with which both Hitler (Frederick) and Churchill (Pilkington) regarded the ideology of communism. Frederick's lawsuits and hard bargaining refer to the process through which Germany arrived at its non-aggression pact with Stalin in 1939.

It is worth noting that the identification of Jones with Tsar Nicholas has now weakened. The Tsar was not in exile- he and his family had been executed by the Bolsheviks in 1918.

Some commentators see the first part of this chapter as a reference to the Russian Civil War of 1918-1921, in which Trotsky led the Red Army (the Bolsheviks) against the counter-revolutionary White Russians, who had help from Britain and France. Mollie, who, being white, we might expect to symbolise the White Russians, stays in her stall; this slightly undermines that reading.

The emphasis on the international suspicion of communism, and the desire of the outside world to see it fail (neighbouring farmers cannot even bring themselves to use the name "Animal Farm", because communism or Bolshevism is so distasteful to them) applies to both the 1920s and the 1930s. Orwell is deft in generalising the allegorical content, and making it unspecific. By letting the force of the narrative take precedence, he succeeds in what he called the fusing of his political purpose and his artistic purpose.

As you read and analyse the events of the story, it is important that you concentrate on what the pigs are doing to distance the farm from Animalism.

They are beginning to corrupt the ideology of fairness and equality. Orwell argues that this is the tendency- and the fundamental problem- with all revolutions. Keeping this concept in your head is essential, but remembering all the historical detail that underpins it is not. Remember, this is English not History. Being able to relate specific episodes in the story to specific historical events is less of a priority for GCSE students – although it may be of high interest to many of your teachers!

Chapter 5

When Mollie is lured back into the service of men, to draw a cart, the last traces of pre-rebellion grace and elegance go with her. This chapter is highly dramatic. It presents the confrontation between Snowball and Napoleon, and the clash of ideologies which leads up to it. Napoleon's ruthlessness is shocking.

Mollie leaves the farm after being "stroked" across the border with Foxwood, and receiving sweeteners of ribbons and sugar lumps.

The Battle of the Cowshed took place in October; the confrontation between Snowball and Napoleon is in the following January. The winter is hard and the ground is frozen. The pigs now make all of the decisions about running the farm, with a vote to ratify them. This is a less democratic way of organising a farm than the democratic debates mentioned in Chapter 3; the less intelligent animals have lost, or given up, their right to speak, and to propose resolutions.

Snowball and Napoleon disagree on everything, because neither is prepared to concede that the other is ever right. Napoleon uses the sheep to disrupt the key moments of Snowball's speeches with their chants of "Four legs good, two legs bad".

Snowball has elaborate plans to improve the farm and make life easier for the animals. His biggest idea is to build a windmill, which would generate electricity for light and heat, and automate the milking. Releasing the animals from some of the grinding work would improve the quality of their lives. The building project would be difficult, and would take a year, but from then on the animals would only have to work for three days a week. Lenin had written, before the 1917 Revolution, that "the socialization of production…….will directly result in an immense increase in productivity of labour, a reduction in working hours, and……..collective and improved labour".

Snowball's response to the acknowledged threat that another attempt to restore Jones to the farm may occur is to send out pigeons to incite rebellions on other farms. This is Trotsky's concept of international socialism; there is no need to defend yourself, if your neighbours are also socialists.

The vision Snowball sets out is true to the principles of rebellion, as Old Major put them; the purpose of the revolution is to end a life of slavery and misery, and to achieve a degree of comfort and dignity by abolishing "hunger and overwork". Significantly, Old Major had objected specifically to Man's theft of the cows' milk, which "should have been breeding up sturdy calves", but "has gone down the throats of our enemies". Napoleon's theft of the milk is a clear and cynical betrayal of the code of Animalism. Snowball's schemes are not designed to give him more power; they are for the benefit of every animal equally.

Before the Meeting in this chapter, Napoleon has been predicting that Snowball's schemes will "come to nothing", while failing to propose any ideas of his own. He has opposed the windmill, and, with the utmost contempt and arrogance, has inspected Snowball's plans for it, "Lifted his leg, urinated…..and walked out without uttering a word".

At other Meetings, Napoleon has said that diverting effort into building a windmill will leave the animals short of food- they will starve. He wants to buy guns and train the animals to use them, to fight off any further attack; here, Orwell is representing Stalin's doctrine of "socialism in one country", as opposed to Trotsky's internationalism.

Orwell has written this chapter with some clever interweaving of the opposed points of view, so that we are as unsure about how the vote will turn out as the animals themselves are, except for one short comment which it may be easy to miss- Napoleon "seemed to be biding his time". This is dark and ominous.

When Snowball refuses to be drowned out by the bleating of the sheep, and sets out his vision of a more comfortable life, it is clear that he has won the argument. Napoleon chooses this moment to let loose his private army, the attack dogs with their "brass-studded collars". They chase Snowball off the farm, in a cartoonish pursuit; Snowball "slipped through a hole in the hedge and was seen no more". The animals notice that Napoleon's dogs obey him much as Jones' dogs used to follow him.

Napoleon has banished his only opponent, so he is now free to abolish the Sunday meetings and debates. From now on, decisions will be taken by a private committee of pigs, run by him; there will be no more voting. The last pretence that Animal Farm is a democracy is being removed; Napoleon will no longer be accountable to the animals. Soon, he will stop appearing as their leader, so that he can live a lazy, whisky-fuelled life, in private comfort, living on the money from the sale of the produce of the working animals' labour (and, eventually, the carcass of Boxer).

This is the start of a totalitarian dictatorship. Boxer feels uncomfortable, and four young pigs squeal a protest until they are intimidated by the growling dogs. These small signs of dissent mark Boxer and these pigs out to be killed later, at the first opportunity, because the regime cannot rely on their unquestioning obedience.

Just as Chapter 3 ended with Squealer redefining the pigs' greed for the milk and the apple crop as self-sacrifice, he reappears here, to defend the indefensible- Napoleon's dismantling of democratic socialism. Again, he uses the word "sacrifice"; he argues that Napoleon will have no pleasure in making all the decisions (how ironic!). Squealer says that no-one is more committed to animal equality than Napoleon- but he cannot risk the animals making the wrong decisions, such as to follow the "criminal" Snowball. Bearing in mind the description of Squealer as the pig who can make black seem white, we understand that the truth beneath his message is that no-one cares about equality **less** than Napoleon.

Snowball has only just been chased into exile, but already Squealer is undermining his reputation; he may have been brave in the Battle of the Cowshed, but his role in it has been "exaggerated".

Again, the threat that any failure in discipline (or obedience to Napoleon) may bring Jones back is one the animals cannot answer. Boxer ducks out of a possible conflict, by inventing and adopting a new, extra slogan- "Napoleon is always right".

The new Sunday meetings separate the animals more distinctly into pigs and the rest. Napoleon sits on a raised platform with Squealer, his bodyguard of the nine dogs, and his latest pen-pusher and songwriter, Minimus. The other pigs are on the platform further behind. The working animals sit on the floor of the barn and face them. It is an arrangement which uses height to confirm the superiority of the pigs, and especially Napoleon. Elitism based on species (pig vs non-pig) is not so far removed from Hitler's concept of racial purity, or from the ethnic cleansing which so often accompanies the rule of dictators.

Minimus is a new character; he has a remarkable ability to write songs and poems for propaganda purposes. His name is a Latin word which means "least" or "smallest". Why do you think Orwell gives him this name? Perhaps it is because what he writes has minimal value, or because it helps the animals to follow the route of least resistance to Napoleon?

The final dramatic twist at the end of Chapter 5 is the announcement that Napoleon *does* want to have the windmill built. The plans are ready. The project will take two years (not the one year Snowball had foreseen); the work will be very hard and there may be a reduction in the animals' "rations" (the military language extends to Napoleon giving orders in a soldierly style). As readers, we are left suspecting that Napoleon sees exhausted and underfed animals as obedient animals; they will not have the energy to rebel against him.

We are reminded, once more, of Old Major's sermon- "Man is…….the root cause of hunger and overwork". Yet here is Napoleon oppressing the animals in precisely the same way. And here are the animals accepting a form of slavery which we know is as bad, or worse, than what they rebelled against. Ironically, they cannot see that for themselves.

Squealer is on hand to explain Napoleon's change of mind, with a sly look, to dispel any sense that the animals' leader may be indecisive. He claims that the windmill was Napoleon's idea; that Snowball had stolen the idea and the plans; and that Napoleon's opposition to it was just tactical. This contradicts what the animals have seen for themselves. But Squealer now has three of the dogs with him; once again, there is no dissent because of the implied threat of violence.

Chapter 6

The windmill is built, slowly and painfully, only for the November storm to destroy the half-finished structure. The pigs are beginning to revise the commandments, in order to avoid being accused of breaking them; they are sleeping in beds (so much for the idea of keeping the farmhouse as a museum!), and Napoleon plans to start trading with humans- something which Old Major insisted animals should never do.

The word "sacrifice", which Squealer had borrowed, and attached, in chapter 5, to Napoleon's developing dictatorship (claiming that he had no desire to make all the decisions!) , recurs here, to describe (accurately) the animals' very hard work, and the threat that the hens will have to give up large numbers of eggs, to raise money for building items. The ironic contrast is telling. The hens' enforced sacrifice or surrender of their eggs was one of the key sources of outrage in Old Major's speech. "Sacrifice" involves giving up something precious, not getting, or taking from others, precisely what you want. Squealer is corrupting language to support the corrupt use of power and privilege.

Sunday working is added to a sixty-hour week. With biting irony, we read that Sunday working is voluntary, but refusing to volunteer will mean that your rations are halved. This is a form of slavery, of the kind Soviet Russia had in the gulags, in hard labour camps, where millions of its own citizens died. It is cynical to pretend that conscription is really a form of volunteering.

The pigs are clever; why, then, can they not invent a more efficient method of breaking up the stones? The answer can only be that they are not interested in making the animals' lives better, or their work easier, as Snowball would have been. The consequence is that Boxer plays a key role in building the windmill (he is by far the strongest animal); he is, in fact, gradually working himself to death. The pigs cannot work out how to use picks and crowbars, here; but, in Chapter 10, they will have learnt to walk on their hind legs and use whips.

The issue of collective animal welfare has disappeared with the exile of Snowball, who had intended the windmill to bring ease and comfort to all the animals. Napoleon has doubled the length of the project (to two years, instead of the one year Snowball had in mind), and made it as harsh as possible, to keep the animals under control.

Old Major had argued that Man had no real interest in animal welfare. We can see for ourselves that, whether or not that was true, Napoleon certainly has none. There should be a point of difference here between human farmers and animals farming; it is concerning that there is none. It is worse when a member of your own species oppresses you.

The animals remain cheerful, whatever burden is put upon them. Because they see only that they are no longer enslaved to human beings, they fail to notice that Napoleon is making their lives at least as bad as they ever were before.   The slave-driver is different- in fact, he is a fellow-animal, which is much worse- but the condition of slavery is the same as before, if not worse.

Napoleon announces that there will be a new policy of trading with humans, to obtain items needed for the farm (including dog biscuits for his private army). The animals think that they can remember passing resolutions against such trade; the four young pigs start to object, and are silenced by the dogs, again. Squealer does his usual tour, to re-programme the animals' minds. He says there was never a resolution against trading and using money; that, as no written record exists, they must have "dreamed" it; and that probably it was a deception started by Snowball. Dreams can be used to control animals- Old Major had used his (imagined or real) dream to motivate the rebellion, and now Squealer tells the animals that their dreams are unreliable.

Unlike the animals, the reader can look and think back. Why not do so yourself now?

You will see that the ban on trading and using money comes from Old Major's speech, in chapter 1, where he warned against the vices of Man-

"No animal must ever live in a house, or sleep in a bed, or wear clothes, or drink alcohol, or smoke tobacco, or touch money, or engage in trade"-

Now, we begin to ask ourselves how long it will be, after one or two of these prohibitions fail, until they are all broken. Orwell wrote about the symmetry of his story; Napoleon's grip on power, and the pigs' metamorphosis into creatures as corrupt and greedy as a combination of human/pig farmers, rise like one side of a see-saw, while the other side- the need to follow the precepts Old Major had set out for a principled and effective post-revolution society- goes down.

The fact that Squealer suggests that the animals are dreaming up rules refers the reader explicitly back to Major and his "dream". Major's "dream" may have been real, or it may have been a piece of invented propaganda, but it motivated the animals to rebel. Now Squealer is using dreams differently- blaming them for the animals' inconvenient reluctance to let go of some deeply held values and principles, which include the innate, instinctive knowledge that humans are to be avoided because they are dangerous and cruel to animals- they kill them for profit.

Jones has now moved away, and there is no longer any threat of an attempt to repossess the farm to restore him to power. The men in the pub hate the socialist ideology of the farm, and persuade themselves that it will fail, but they grudgingly concede that, however distasteful it may be, it has a valid new name. Just as the old Russia had been re-named the USSR, with the word "socialist" in its title (the full name is

United Soviet Socialist Republic), so "Animal Farm" now has the key word "animal" (for Animalism) in its name.

As soon as the pigs start trading (using Mr Whymper to represent them), they break more of Old Major's injunctions; they move into the farmhouse (which the animals had resolved to keep as a museum, in chapter 2) and start sleeping in the beds. Clover finds that the fourth commandment has been changed, so that it is not sleeping in beds which is an offence, but sleeping in a bed "with sheets".

This is the first instance of Squealer rewriting the rules to make the "Unalterable Law", or the rules of society, fit what suits the pigs. Old Major had talked about an unalterable law, but, for the pigs who survived him, there is no such concept.

It is morally wrong and undemocratic to make these changes without consent, and it insults the (low) intelligence of the animals. The pigs know that they can outsmart the other animals, and exploit them.

Once more, Squealer- accompanied by two or three of the vicious dogs- defends the use of beds, as a means of keeping Jones away. The animals do not know what the reader knows- that Jones is no longer planning to return. Having confirmed the animals' gullibility in this way, the pigs then award themselves an extra hour in bed each day. This further emphasises the class and privilege gap, the laziness of the pigs, their selfishness, their lack of conscience, and how far they have already betrayed Major's vision of a socialist collective in which all animals are genuinely equal.

The storm which destroys the (incomplete) windmill wakes up the hens. They are "squawking with terror because they had all dreamed simultaneously of hearing a gun go off". Just as Major's dream came true, their nightmare- another type of dream- will become real, very soon, with the violent deaths by execution in the next chapter.

Chapter 6 ends with Napoleon orchestrating the response to the damage to the windmill. He blames Snowball for destroying it- conveniently ignoring the real cause, the storm- because creating and demonising a dark and powerful enemy is a more effective way of motivating and controlling the animals than admitting the true, natural cause of the destruction. A nation which believes a strong enemy is out to destroy it will remain united and determined to resist, whatever the hardships. The historical parallel is Hitler's invasion of Russia.

Napoleon makes the exiled Snowball seem more dangerous, by pronouncing a death sentence on him (for alleged treachery), and by offering a reward for capturing him- a military decoration, and a large quantity of apples. He must know that the apples are safe, because Snowball is very unlikely to try to return.

This episode once again gives the chapter a strong ending. Generally, the chapter endings are to do with corrupt or violent behaviour. In chapter 1, Jones shoots his gun indiscriminately in the dark. Chapter 2 ends with Napoleon taking the milk, and Chapter 3 closes with Squealer defending that theft. Jones' gun reappears at the end of Chapter 4, where the sheep is buried. The end of Chapters 5 and 6 show us Napoleon manipulating the passive and easily led animals in his own extreme pursuit of power- an error which Napoleon Bonaparte, Hitler and Stalin were all guilty of.

Chapter 7

The process of reconstruction starts, although the winter is hard and cold; the animals are determined to prove to the outside world that they can modernise the farm by building a better windmill. This time the walls will be three feet thick, instead of 18 inches; so twice as much stone will be needed. The plan to build the windmill within a set deadline (Snowball's one year, Napoleon's two) reminds us of Stalin's five-year plans to centralise and improve national economic performance and production. They were accompanied by extreme hardship for the labouring people of Russia.

In chapter 6, Napoleon had sold part of the winter supply of corn and hay (for dog biscuits etc), so there is a food shortage, made worse by not storing the potatoes properly. The Russian resistance to Hitler continued in 1942 despite the deliberate starvation, by the German Army, of the populations of Stalingrad and Moscow.

Napoleon orchestrates a form of presentational propaganda to give the impression (to Whymper, and, through him, to the outside world) that the animals are well fed.

Napoleon signs a contract to supply 400 eggs per week until the summer, to buy emergency supplies of grain and meal. The hens protest that to take the eggs is "murder"; they lay their eggs on the rafters, from where they smash on the floor. This is a reference to Stalin's programme to reform agricultural production by eliminating the kulaks.

The response is brutal; the hens are starved into submission, with their exclusion from feeding enforced by Napoleon's dogs. Nine hens die.

Napoleon wants to sell a stock of timber to either Frederick or Pilkington, both of whom want to buy it. This reflects the international position of the USSR in the earlier part of the Second World War. Both Hitler's Germany and the West wanted Russia as an ally; in the end, Russia was deceived by Hitler's non-aggression pact. Orwell alludes to this when Frederick buys the timber with false currency- betraying the trust of Animal Farm, and deceiving it.

The hens' rebellion (the kulaks) and the more general unease among the animals, bred of low food supplies, means that "for the first time since the expulsion of Jones there was something resembling a rebellion"; this represents the state of agricultural Russia in the 1930s.

Napoleon will react to this discontent, and the slightest possibility of a popular uprising, with repression of shocking cruelty- the "show trials" of animals which, terrified, admit to various crimes, including helping Snowball, the enemy of the state, who is alleged to prowl and sabotage the farm at night (of course, this is a lie). Those animals will be executed at the meeting, publicly, by Napoleon's dogs.

This chapter is full of lies and misinformation. The human beings spread lies about the failure of the socialist farm; Napoleon misrepresents the food shortages; the hens which have been starved to death for defying Napoleon's orders are said to have died of disease; Snowball's alleged whereabouts are an excuse for Napoleon's indecisiveness over the timber sale; Squealer lies about Snowball's alliance with Jones (past) and Frederick (present), and says there are documents- conveniently, only just discovered-which prove that Snowball is a traitor. Squealer has the nerve to claim that Snowball tried to lose the Battle of the Cowshed, and that Napoleon had, heroically, bitten Jones- an outright lie, which we can check by referring to the Battle, in Chapter 4. Far from being a "heroic Leader", Napoleon was not even on the battlefield.

Orwell is showing us two things here- the tendency for totalitarian regimes to lie, with one lie leading to a bigger one, and lying becoming a habitual propaganda tool; and the habit they have of rewriting history, to suit themselves.

Making Snowball the author of every insidious attack, and making him the object of fear and paranoia, is possible, because he is not there to defend himself, and it is also convenient for Napoleon.

Stalin demonised Trotsky in much the same way, and those who disappeared in Stalin's purges were given a different role in the Soviet history which the state created. Like Snowball, they were condemned for crimes they had not committed. While the threat of Jones returning helped to keep the animals in line, earlier, and to enable Napoleon to organise the farm as he wanted to, the allegations that Snowball is an active enemy, who invades their territory, unseen, when they are asleep, creates a threat which unites the animals in their common purpose, and distracts them from their own sufferings.

When Boxer questions – however mildly- the "truth" about Snowball which Squealer now presents, Squealer gives him "a very ugly look". Boxer's resistance to propaganda is always weak, because he is inclined to accept what he is told, and is a paragon of hard work, self-sacrifice and obedience. Nevertheless, Squealer has marked him out now as an enemy of the state, after his silent worries about the loss of democracy in Chapter 5, when voting was abolished (although Boxer accepted the pigs' use of beds). This is a clue to how he will be treated in chapter 9, which itself fulfils Old Major's prophecy from Chapter 1 about how Boxer will die.

Half way through, Chapter 7 lays aside this theme of the use of propaganda, to give us the dramatic scene of the show trials and executions, and then the animals' reaction to it. We are just past half way through the narrative, and Orwell subjects us to a real and lasting shock. The ideology and the optimism of the rebellion evaporate in the face of the hard reality of how dictators exercise power.

Napoleon orders an assembly in the late afternoon. Both the unusual timing and the fact that he is in full military attire, having awarded himself both medals, give the animals a sense that "some terrible thing was about to happen". He sets the dogs on to their prey with a "high-pitched whimper"- the same descriptive phrase which had set the dogs chasing Snowball away in Chapter 5.

The dogs attack the four pigs, and they try to attack Boxer, who is too big for them. The pigs, who have been guilty only of a mildly unpig-like interest in democracy, suddenly confess that they have been plotting with Snowball to betray the farm to Frederick; the dogs tear their throats out. They are followed by the three rebellious hens, a goose, and three sheep- none of whom have done anything particularly treacherous. Orwell extends the process with more, unspecified

"confessions and executions", "until there was a pile of corpses……
and the air was heavy with the smell of blood".

Reading this, we wonder why an animal (or anyone) would confess to
something which is obviously completely untrue, as these four pigs do.
Have they been told they must confess, or die? That would be bad
enough, and it would imply that Napoleon then planned to kill them
anyway. Or do they confess, knowing that they will be killed anyway?
That would be chilling. And then other animals make other
confessions, having already seen that any confession is followed by
immediate execution by dog!!

The scene is a disturbing piece of cold-blooded killing. Perhaps it is a
representation not just of Stalin's show trials, but also of the murder of
the defenceless Tsar and his family, on the orders of the Bolshevik
leaders, in 1918.

Eleven animals are killed, plus others which are not given a number-
in the space of just two paragraphs.

The violence here is very different from the comic-book coming to
blows in the Battle of the Cowshed.

The narrative expresses the animals' shock; the animals recognise, as
we do, that no animal had killed another animal, after the rebellion,
until now. The killings tear up the sixth commandment, and strike at
the core principle of social cohesion which lies at the heart of
"animalism".

Boxer cannot understand or explain the mass murders, but prescribes
himself the usual cure- more work. Clover cannot express her
thoughts, so Orwell writes a long, sad passage which describes both
the idyllic setting of the farm and the countryside and her sense of
grief and betrayal, now that the noble motivation for the rebellion has
become so perverted. Even so, she will not question the authority of

Napoleon, because the overall priority is still "to prevent the return of the human beings"; any price is worth paying, to achieve that.

The animals, cowed, cold and traumatised, comfort themselves with a mournful, grief-stricken singing of "Beasts of England". Once more, Squealer appears, to finish the Chapter, with the intrusion of more propaganda- this time, a decree that "Beasts of England" is banned, because the executions of the "internal enemy" have ended the process of revolution. Minimus has composed a short and anodyne song to replace it. "Beasts of England" is the animals' last connection with the ideology and noble principles of the rebellion.

It is a nostalgic refuge for them, a comfort blanket of sorts. But such comfort, in the pigs' opinion, encourages wishful thinking and disloyalty. Napoleon has now secured his position as a totalitarian dictator, by eliminating his opponents.

The move from revolution to after the revolution involves the working animals giving up the hope that things are going to be better in the future, and accepting them as they are. The object of the new song is Animal Farm- the state- not the beasts themselves. Minimus has produced a platitude which seeks merely to reinforce the state of things as they are; the ambition for change and improvement is to be discouraged, because such a desire can only serve to destabilise the dictator.

We should remember what Hobbes had said about the "social contract"- that citizens surrender their rights, and agree to be governed, in exchange for being kept safe. When a dictator, king or president stops caring about the safety of his people, and starts killing them, he is no longer a legitimate leader. Atrocities like Napoleon's executions of animals should lead to an uprising which removes him from power, but the animals are too weak to rebel against him.

Chapter 8

Just as the breaking of the fourth commandment was obscured, by adding a few words to it, the sixth commandment has now mysteriously been modified with an extra two words, making it "No animal shall kill any other animal **without cause**".

This chapter will end with another redrawing of another commandment, the fifth, after the pigs have developed a taste for alcohol. It will be another irreversible step on their road to betraying all the principles of animalism.

The chapter deals with two main topics; the developing of a personality cult around the "Leader" of the totalitarian state, and, alongside that political/historical/philosophical subject, there is the practical task of the rebuilding of the windmill.

Orwell also continues to reflect on the nature and the effects of political propaganda; and events in this chapter partly allude to the historical events which led to the non-aggression pact between Stalin and Hitler in 1939.

Rebuilding the windmill, using twice as much stone for the walls, is very hard to do, and it takes another year. With even more work than before, the building is complete in the autumn, although the machinery is yet to be bought.

The narrative explains- ironically- that "nothing short of explosives" will destroy the new windmill. The animals still believe that the project will be for their benefit, because the original plan, formulated by Snowball, was for the windmill to generate electricity for heat, light and mechanised farming. They are jubilant when they think about the "enormous difference" it will make to them.

The animals here are like the Russian people in the 1930s and afterwards, undergoing a huge project to modernise and automate their factories and industry- a programme bedevilled by slow progress, inadequate food supply, and an attempt by the authorities (like Squealer's here) to use statistics to claim that life is already better, when every animal/citizen instinctively knows that it isn't.

Napoleon misjudges the character of Frederick, whom the other animals "feared and hated". Frederick is a German name, and we are expected to think of Frederick as Hitler in this Chapter. Frederick misleads Napoleon into believing that he has no intention of attacking Animal Farm; Hitler invaded Russia in 1941 after giving reassurances that he would not.

Frederick deceives Napoleon by buying the timber with forged five pound notes- worthless currency. The money for the timber is needed to enable the machinery for the windmill to be bought; in other words, for the programme of industrial modernisation to be completed. This piece of cheating puts Animal Farm on a war footing, and the attack (or invasion) takes place the next day. Napoleon has passed the death sentence on Frederick (as he had on Snowball) and threatens to boil him alive if he captures him.

The second battle is much larger than the first, the Battle of the Cowshed in chapter 4. Jones had five men and one gun; Frederick brings fifteen men and six guns. The animals give up much ground, including the windmill, which the human attackers demolish with explosives (as the narrative has foreshadowed).

The attack focuses on the windmill, which represents everything the animals are working towards, because Hitler wanted to destroy the socialist state of Russia; the battle between communism and Fascism is an ideological one.

With comic irony, Napoleon declares that the walls of the windmill are too thick to be knocked down. Are there amusing echoes here of the children's story of the three little pigs and their houses built of straw, wood and brick?

Benjamin, the donkey, is his usual detached, laconic self (like Eeyore in the Winnie the Pooh stories). The mindless blowing up of the windmill animates the animals to fight back; the battle is "savage, bitter", although Orwell does not describe it with the immediacy and close-up horror of the executions in chapter 7. A cow, three sheep and two geese are killed, but the human army is driven away by the dogs, and there are two days of celebration, to commemorate the "Battle of the Windmill".

Squealer is now appearing regularly as the bearer of Napoleon's messages; Napoleon cannot be bothered to maintain a personal relationship with the animals. In chapter 7, Squealer had started referring to him as "our heroic Leader". Napoleon's appearances are much less frequent now because he has no opponents, and can rule by intimidation, not democratic consent. He wants to be feared, not admired, as he becomes more corrupted by power and by the indulgent comforts he can take for himself.

Napoleon has added to his parade of dogs a cockerel (we think of them as a peculiarly French, and therefore Napoleonic, bird), which trumpets his arrival wherever he goes, on his rare- perhaps twice-monthly- public appearances.

Along with this distancing, Napoleon now has an official title- "our Leader, Comrade Napoleon". He also has a string of titles which the pigs have invented for him- Father of All Animals, Terror of Mankind, Protector of the Sheepfold, Ducklings' Friend. They are exaggerated, and ironically self-regarding, as is the new poem which Minimus composes under the title "Comrade Napoleon".

Orwell slyly undermines its pomposity by giving Napoleon the accolade "Lord of the swill-bucket" in the first verse of the poem. The dictator's minions have lost any sense of irony or proportion which they may once have had. Napoleon arranges for the poem to be written on the barn wall opposite the seven commandments, together with a portrait of himself "in profile". As the animals do not have the means of producing a statue of him, this is the next best thing. It elevates his importance to equal the importance of the commandments. The rebuilt windmill is not to be seen as the animals' achievement; it is to be called "Napoleon Mill".

Napoleon is vain enough to be seduced by his own legend. He is duped by Frederick, who buys the timber with forged banknotes, but, at first, the pigs "were in ecstasies over Napoleon's cunning". In a sublimely deluded display of arrogance, he calls "another special meeting" where the animals file past slowly, as he "reposes on a bed of straw", wearing his military decorations, and shows off the money. This is like an audience with a decadent Roman Emperor (Caligula? Nero?).

In revealing, one paragraph later, that the banknotes are worthless, Orwell punctures the balloon of Napoleon's pomposity immediately, and with maximum comic effect. Increasingly self-absorbed and paranoid, Napoleon has his bed guarded at night, with a dog at each corner, and he has a "young pig named Pinkeye" tasting his food, in case it is poisoned. We are rather hoping that it will be!

Squealer stirs up admiration for "the superior quality of Napoleon's mind". He recites to the hungry animals lists of statistics about "production", which the animals accept, even though they are clearly invented. He takes no part in the battle- he is too important to Napoleon to be put at risk- and presents the fact that the animals have lost the windmill, but retained the "sacred soil of Animal Farm", as a "victory…..(a) mighty thing". The elaborate celebrations after the battle achieve the cynical aim of making the animals forget the forged banknotes and Napoleon's humiliating defeat by Frederick in that regard.

Squealer continues to assassinate Snowball's character, saying that he was not decorated for his part in the Battle of the Cowshed, and was in fact "censured for showing cowardice in the battle". Again, we only have to refer back to Chapter 4 to remind ourselves of the facts, but the animals, who cannot do that, are persuaded "that their memories had been at fault".

It is sinister (and it casts doubt even in our minds for a moment or two) that the lies about Snowball's continuing sabotage of the crops are legitimised by the suicide of a gander, who "had confessed his guilt to Squealer"; it seems that Squealer's orders are to have as many individual animals put to death as is necessary to keep the animals as a whole misled and under control.

Chapter 8 concludes with a comic scene, in which the pigs drink Jones' whisky, and Napoleon suffers from a hangover so bad that they think he is dying. Orwell goes beyond mere humour here- he is writing satirically, using the pigs' experience of going too far, and drinking too much, to show us their limitations, silliness and folly.

It is amusing, naturally, that Orwell's pigs should show an unregulated appetite, because pigs are greedy (just as their inherent laziness has already found expression in their one-hour lie-ins in the mornings).

Napoleon's 'dying' pronouncement is that "the drinking of alcohol was to be punished by death", because he wants to save other animals from suffering his own hangover, which lasts for almost two days. Having survived it, Napoleon has an about turn and a new project- to sow barley and manufacture beer on the farm, not for the benefit of all the animals, but only for the ruling class, the pigs, and particularly for himself (he will be allotted four pints of beer per day).

The gap between a drunken Napoleon now, and the drunken Mr Jones at the start of the tale, is a small one. Squealer is caught changing the fifth commandment from a prohibition on alcohol to "No animal shall drink alcohol **to excess**". Napoleon's own definition of excess, for alcohol as for violence and terror, is not just that of a selfish dictator; it is also that of a greedy pig. Squealer falls off the ladder because he, like the other pigs, has developed a taste for whisky, and is drunk. The pigs' liking for whisky is so strong that they will sell Boxer for it, in the next chapter.

Only Benjamin understands what Squealer has been doing, under cover of darkness; he does not explain it to the other animals. It is as if Orwell is telling us that if we cannot see the way the authorities are (constantly and secretly) redefining the values and rules of the society we live in, and we passively allow them to do whatever they like, without questioning it, or noticing it, we deserve what we get.

Chapter 8 has moved the farm even further from Old Major's guiding principles. The pigs now live in the farmhouse, sleep in beds, drink alcohol, touch money and engage in trade- all signs of corruption, because they blur the fundamental distinction between the animal species and the human.

Now is a good time to go back and find the sentence in Chapter One where Old Major lists his warnings.

What ban is left for the pigs to break? Only the rules that animals must not wear clothes, and must not smoke tobacco. As readers, we are now waiting for those last taboos to be broken; we know that, as soon as that occurs, the revolution will be dead.

Chapter 9

The action in this chapter is in the second half- Boxer's collapse, and his removal from the farm, for a grim death which fulfils yet another of old Major's prophecies.

The first part of the chapter develops the class distinctions on the farm, the elitism of the pigs, the perversion of truth through more and more outrageous propaganda, and the animals becoming so hungry that even Moses the raven, with his escapist vision of a better life only after death, returns after "several years". His reappearance is proof that the revolution has failed; the animals are back in exactly the same deprived and exploited position as at the outset of the rebellion, in chapter 2. The groundwork for the rebellion had included the pigs arguing "very hard" to convince the animals that Sugarcandy Mountain (heaven) did not exist, so that they could be motivated to revolutionary action, instead of continuing to accept their hardships as the natural order of society.

Moses had been Jones' "especial pet", fed on beer-soaked crusts of bread, because his tales of heaven helped to keep the animals from becoming militant or disobedient. Now, the pigs, just like Jones had done, allow Moses to speak to the animals, and feed him with beer; he is an anti-revolutionary asset for those who are in charge and who want to stay in control.

Food is scarcer than ever, during another hard winter, but the pigs and the dogs do not have their rations reduced; the cuts, or, as Squealer calls it, "readjustment", only applies, ironically and cynically, to the working animals. He tells them they have more food than before the rebellion, but the fact that he reads the figures out in "a shrill rapid voice" shows that even he cannot make a case for these particular lies.

Napoleon has sired thirty-one young pigs- making use of all of the four sows on the farm. Not only do these extra animals have to be fed; a schoolroom has to be budgeted for and built, for their use only; pigs must be made way for when they meet other animals; only pigs can wear ribbons on Sundays; the farm's shopping list is longer now, with the addition of lamp oil and candles for the farmhouse, and sugar for Napoleon. We see that most of the benefit from the animals' work is being directed to the comfort of the pigs alone, not the animals collectively- in other words, animalism has been suppressed in favour, once more, of capitalism. The pigs feed on the labour of the other animals, while they themselves do no work, do not yield milk, and do not lay eggs.

To fund the pigs' lifestyle, even more hay, potatoes and eggs are sold, so that the other animals' rations are reduced in both December and February, but the pigs are getting fatter. They are cooking barley, and brewing beer, but they have no intention to share it with the working animals.

While Orwell's narrative voice can tell us the facts and the truth objectively, the animals are subjected to ever more outrageous tricks and deceptions, designed to disguise the inequalities the pigs are imposing on them. There are "more songs, more speeches, more processions", in order to preoccupy the animals, and distract them from their hunger.

Napoleon orders that there must be a military-style parade round the perimeter of the farm every week, in a strict formation (the cockerel, then pigs, horses, cows, sheep, poultry), with the dogs on the flanks. This is rather like exercise hour in a prison or a concentration camp.

There is irony in the naming of these parades as a Spontaneous Demonstration, because there is nothing spontaneous about them. They waste time and the animals are cold during them. It is doubly ironic- and sad- that the animals find them "comforting" because the parades remind them that "they were truly their own masters….the work they did was for their own benefit".

In fact, the animals are celebrating their own exploitation by the pigs, because they cannot see it for what it is. There are only ever a few complaints, and those are only expressed "when no pigs or dogs were near", because freedom of speech (like the promise that, under animalism, there would be more than enough food) no longer exists.

Some of the methods of repression are different, but we are in no doubt that the animals' lives are worse now than they were when Jones ran the farm.

The pretence that all animals are equal should not survive the pigs' treatment of the working animals. To add insult to injury, the farm is then declared a Republic, with Napoleon (the only candidate) "elected unanimously" as President. A one-candidate election is a sign of a totalitarian regime.

Even without any opposition, Napoleon is still ordering Squealer to revise Snowball's position in the official history of the farm- he is now cast as the leader of Jones' attack in the Battle of the Cowshed, while his injuries are said to be not from Jones' gun but from Napoleon's teeth. The propaganda machine grinds on, leaving nothing positive about Snowball on the record. This mirrors the way Stalin's political opponents were airbrushed out of official records and history.

Boxer is eleven years old. He had suffered lasting injuries in the most recent battle- a split hoof, and a dozen shotgun pellets in his back leg. His hoof takes time to heal, but he then works harder than ever before, because there is the schoolhouse to build, as well as the windmill. Boxer's age and the lack of nutrition mean he is not so strong; he is pushing himself to do too much, because of his determination to solve all problems by working harder.

At the age of twelve, horses are due to retire; retirement holds out the promise of rest and ample food. Boxer's twelfth birthday is imminent, "in the late summer". It is midsummer, and his birthday is only a month away, when Boxer collapses, with a damaged lung. Clover had foreshadowed this, when she told Boxer (in the first paragraph of this chapter) not to work too hard, because "a horse's lungs do not last for ever".

He knows, at once, that his working life is over; we know that no animal has yet managed to retire. We also have, at the back of our mind, a prediction which Old Major had made; during his speech, he had addressed Boxer, directly, in Chapter 1-

"You, Boxer, the very day that those great muscles of yours lose their power, Jones will sell you to the knacker, who will cut your throat and boil you down for the foxhounds".

We remember, too, that, in Chapter 7, when Boxer was reluctant to accept Squealer's lie that Snowball was Jones' secret agent, Squealer "cast a very ugly look at Boxer". In that chapter, too, the show trial had started with a dog trying to attack Boxer. Napoleon had "appeared to change countenance, and sharply ordered Boxer to let the dog go".

Because we recognise that Napoleon (the drinker) is no different from Jones (the drinker), we know that we could substitute Napoleon for Jones in Old Major's prophecy; and that Boxer is a threat to the regime, because of his strength and his very slight reluctance to accept everything he is told without the slightest questioning.

Orwell has managed our response so that we do not expect Boxer to survive to retirement; this is not a happy ever after fairy tale, but "a fairy story". We know that in the earliest days of animalism Boxer would have been saved, if he had been injured like this. Now, he is an easy and defenceless target for Napoleon, who has never missed an opportunity to eliminate anyone who could oppose him. Stalin exiled anyone who was labelled "an enemy of the state" to hard labour camps, where they would die of malnutrition and overwork. Napoleon has pre-planned the same fate for Boxer; we know that Boxer is loyal to a fault, and deserves nothing but gratitude.

Squealer tells Clover and Benjamin that Comrade Napoleon is arranging for Boxer to go to hospital in the village. The animals worry- rightly, perhaps- that a human vet might not be trustworthy- they "did not like to think of their sick comrade in the hands of human beings". They are aware, too, that the animals who have left the farm- Mollie and Snowball- have never returned. We know what the animals do not- that what is more dangerous for Boxer than the vet is Napoleon's plan for him.

Orwell adds to the pathos by reporting a conversation in which Boxer tells Clover that he hopes to live for another three years, and learn the alphabet. Even these modest and harmless ambitions are to be denied.

"The van came to take him away" when Benjamin and Clover, his protectors, were at work, two days later. The van has "lettering on its side"; Benjamin reads the wording out, "in the midst of a deadly silence".

The van belongs to the Horse Slaughterer- the knacker of whom Old Major had spoken. Warned by the other animals, Boxer tries to escape from inside the van, but he lacks the strength to do so, and, like Snowball, who, in chapter 5, "was seen no more",Boxer "was never seen again".

The account of Boxer's death, and the way Napoleon and Squealer exploit it for political and propaganda purposes, is devastating. Squealer says that the vet had bought the van from the knacker, but not painted his name on it; is "almost unbelievable" that "any animal could be so stupid" as to think Napoleon would have sent Boxer to his death. Napoleon regrets that "it had not been possible" to bring Boxer's body back for burial; we know that this is because it has been used, already, for glue and animal feed! Ironically, the animals are not so stupid as to misunderstand whose van it was, but they are stupid enough to be persuaded by Squealer that Boxer "had died happy".

We feel that it is almost unbelievable that any animal could be so cynical as to exploit the working animals' lack of intelligence in this way.

Napoleon says that, instead of a funeral for Boxer, there will be a "memorial banquet"- held by the pigs (and therefore excluding the working animals). On that day, a crate of whisky arrives; the dinner ends with drunken fighting. The inference is that Napoleon has paid for the whisky with the money for Boxer's carcass. In proving himself Boxer's mortal enemy and assassin, and selling him for money, Napoleon has broken- grotesquely- the second, fifth and sixth commandments, all at the same time.

Chapter 10

Chapter 10 opens with a list of those who, after some years, have died. Clover is fourteen, but has not retired, although horses are supposed to stop working at the age of twelve. Napoleon and Squealer are horribly fat. The farm has more animals on it than ever before, and it is more prosperous and larger, with the windmill complete; but the windmill is used to mill corn, not to generate electricity and give the animals a shorter working week. Napoleon, hypocritically, says that happiness lies in "working hard and living frugally"- neither of which he has ever done himself.

The pigs and dogs have become a petit bourgeoisie of administrators, creating paperwork, which they then burn! They have found that written records would get in the way of the constant revision of history which it suits them to enforce, as they devote their real energies to maintaining their position of power. Squealer is still reciting lists of figures, claiming constant improvement; they cannot be disproved, if there are no written records from the past to compare them with.

This "superstructure" of non-productive pigs and dogs guarantees hardship for the proletarian working animals. But their sense of satisfaction in being the only Animal Farm means that the idea of rebelling again still does not enter their minds. Instead, they believe that, at some point in the future, humans will be driven out of England altogether.

This is a case of misplaced loyalty, and faulty thinking. Orwell undermines the animals' position in the narrative, when he draws our attention to the source of their hope- whatever their sufferings, "No creature among them went upon two legs. All animals were equal". This takes us back to the seven commandments, which are listed in Chapter 2.

Animalism is barely still alive, because so many of the commandments have been allowed to be broken.

In making Mr Whymper their friend, buying two fields from Pilkington, and trading with Frederick, the pigs have broken the first. In allowing Napoleon to kill Boxer and his other victims, the animals have found the second is untrue; Napoleon has broken the sixth. The pigs have long drunk whisky and beer, and slept in beds (commandments four and five). The selfish pre-eminence of the pigs and the dogs shows that, in practice, the seventh commandment has been disregarded. This leaves only the wearing of clothes as the last shred of animalism which remains intact; it is the last point which distinguishes animals from Mankind.

Old Major had argued that animals would no longer suffer "misery and slavery" if they drove out the humans, who exploit them for their labour. Look back to what Old Major said, and you can now substitute the words "Pigs" or "Napoleon" for "Man". The only saving grace is that the young animals are not killed for meat. Major's warning that "we must not come to resemble (Man)….do not adopt his vices" has been ignored, except for the minor points of smoking tobacco and wearing clothes.

Orwell's aim, in this final chapter, is to decapitate the experiment of animalism with a final coup de grace. First of all, the pigs- Squealer, a long line of other pigs, and then Napoleon- learn to walk on two legs.

Napoleon is "haughty" and "majestically upright". This is the most shocking possible rejection of the principle that all animals are equal. It is provocative, and the equivalent of a declaration of war on the other animals- because, as the first commandment said, whatever goes upon two legs is an enemy.

The sheep's altered chant of "Four legs good, two legs better" is a bastardised revision of the familiar, reassuring "Four legs good, two legs bad". The Napoleon regime has such an iron grip that it can, in an instant, introduce a change of emphasis which makes something which has always been accepted as bad (morally wrong) into something "better" (morally desirable).

The sinister power of the gesture lies in the fact that, in walking on their hind legs, the pigs are repudiating their own species, and alienating themselves from animalism, with a deliberately hostile affront to every common belief the animals have ever shared.

All that is needed to complete Napoleon's metamorphosis into the new Jones is a whip, clothing, and a newspaper to read. Inevitably, in this chapter, all of these changes occur, close together; while Napoleon, "with a pipe in his mouth", has now broken the last of Old Major's principles, about smoking tobacco.

The wearing of clothes kills off the third commandment, and Orwell takes the opportunity to demolish the all-important seventh commandment too. Even the pigs can no longer pretend that all animals are equal, or that they have not broken all the other commandments. Therefore, the pigs have erased the whole of the old list, and replaced it with the appalling truth they have themselves created- that "some animals are more equal than others".

This embeds the principle of inequality; of exploitation; of totalitarian control; of disregard for the individual.

The pigs' desire to be accepted by the neighbouring farmers, as friends with shared interests, motivates the drinks party in the farmhouse, which also represents the Teheran conference of 1943, where Churchill, Roosevelt and Stalin agreed on an allied strategy for the remainder of the war against Hitler.

The capitalist human farmers approve of the efficient way Animal Farm is run; they will adopt its practices, themselves, in order to run down their own animals even more, exploit them more, and extract greater production from them, while feeding them less. Ironically, the animalism experiment has made the animals objectively worse off than ever before- it has proved utterly futile.

Pilkington/Churchill expresses a desire for reconciliation with Russia, setting aside his concerns about the destabilising effects of communism.

More importantly, Pilkington observes that all farmers- whether they are humans or pigs- share the same interests and concerns. Old Major had insisted that the interests of humans and animals were always opposed- "Never listen when they tell you that Man and the animals have a common interest….all Men are enemies". Pilkington congratulates the pigs on their method of tackling the class system- by exploiting the underclass openly, and not pretending that all animals are equal.

Napoleon/Stalin responds to Pilkington, stating that he has no desire to incite rebellion on other farms (he wants to pursue peace, not radical international socialism, as Trotsky would have done). While Animal Farm is a co-operative, he will now suppress the use of the term "comrade" (which implies equality), and the flag has been changed; the hoof and horn have gone. In Chapter 3, Snowball had explained that the hoof and horn "signified the future Republic of the Animals which would arise when the human race had been finally overthrown". Removing them from the flag shows that Animal Farm no longer entertains any ambitions for revolution, or for better rights for animals. And Napoleon is abolishing the very name of Animal Farm-reverting to the original, "correct" name of The Manor Farm. The whole era of animalism is being wiped away, in a return to the authoritarian, elitist society of the years before the Russian revolution.

The argument between Napoleon and Pilkington- "each had played an ace of spades simultaneously"- shows that mutual suspicion will continue between capitalist and socialist states, whatever they may say.

But more important than this quarrel is the fact that, to the animals, there is now nothing to distinguish the pigs from the men; the champions of inequality are all around them, and they hold all the power and all the aces.

Orwell wrote that his intention was to end the tale "on a loud note of discord", and that he completed this chapter just after the Teheran Conference; he wanted to express his instinct that the peace and accord between the USSR and the Western allies was an uneasy one, which it would be impossible to maintain.

"Animal Farm" on film

A 1954 cartoon animation of the book was the first animated feature film made in Britain. It was paid for by the Central Intelligence Agency in the USA, which wanted to promote anti-communist entertainment. A second version using animations and actors appeared in 1999. It is 90 minutes long, compared with 70 minutes for the earlier film.

Neither of these versions tackles the violence faithfully, and they both change the bleak ending. Orwell shows us, in the story, how difficult it will be to overthrow Napoleon and his dynasty; the outlook for the oppressed animals is hopeless. The films make the ending much more optimistic.

A practical difficulty for the film director is the need to treat the story first and foremost as a story. A feature film is not a natural medium for explaining the symbolism and allegorical meanings, or for making the historical references clear to the viewer. The later version is successful in its presentation of the power of propaganda. Neither film manages to make the human characters as significant as Orwell intended them to be, and the point of view does not translate to the cinema screen very comfortably or convincingly.

The appeal of the earlier film lies largely in its own enjoyment of the animation techniques it uses- a great deal of time and space is devoted to animals marching or harvesting, which are minor elements of the written text. Benjamin assumes the role of Clover. Whymper is not a solicitor, but a trader and the owner of the horse "death wagon". There is no place for Mrs Jones, and neither Frederick nor Pilkington are clearly identified.

The windmill is only destroyed once- by Jones, using dynamite.

There are only five commandments. Napoleon is gluttonous rather than terrifying, and the "fat pig" Squealer lacks menace. The order of events is changed early on, with the Battle of the Cowshed taking place before the commandments are published. The show trial executions are done off-camera, and the treatment of the content of Old Major's speech and of the use of propaganda is weak.

While the film is faithful to the book, in showing the pigs walking upright and being like Jones, these scenes lack power and resonance, because the film version invents a new ending. Animals on other farms, outraged at the rejection of the commandment that all animals are equal, arrive to drive Napoleon out, and he is defenceless because his dogs are drunk.

The style of the film concentrates on its visual impact, and the music soundtrack. There is very little dialogue, and not much narration.

The opening credits tell us that the film is based on Orwell's "memorable fable". This implies- accurately- that this film version will take a fairly simple approach to the story telling. The idea that a first revolution then leads to another one, to remove the corruption it has given rise to, is a fable of a sort- but it does not do real justice to the historical and philosophical references which lie at the heart of Orwell's version.

The allegorical dimension, the references to Russia and Stalin, and the ruthlessness of the fascism of the pigs in the original are less important than the way the film explores the potential for animation to tell a story in an economical way. Much is not said, but is represented through visual clues; the direction which Orwell provides through his narrative persona is absent.

The 1954 film should be relied on less than most "films of the book", as a study aid, because its ambitions and aims are distinctly different from those of the written text.

The altered ending (especially if the CIA funding influenced it) is a warning to a highly militarised totalitarian state after Stalin had died (in 1953); the ten years since Orwell wrote the story have lent a rather different context to the politics of this film version.

In the later film, the narrator is the dog, Jessie- although, in Orwell's story, she has died before the start of chapter 10. The animals' abject suffering under Napoleon is not a constant, throbbing pain, as it is in Orwell's text.

The 1999 film, directed by John Stephenson, has a screenplay which adds details- Jones owes Pilkington money, and has a one-night stand with Mrs Pilkington. Old Major dies because he is hit by Jones' gunshot- not of old age; and he is not buried, but butchered by Jones.

Pilkington's character is changed and expanded. He is not Orwell's "easy-going gentleman farmer", but a violent, angry, unsympathetic bully, who introduces Napoleon to whisky, and conducts the trading for which Orwell has Mr Whymper (who does not appear in the film). The Battle of the Cowshed is led by Pilkington and Frederick, not Jones; and the windmill is blown up by Jones, not destroyed in a storm. The windmill itself is no more than a pile of junk- it has no useful purpose.

Among the episodes the film leaves out are Mollie's departure, Napoleon's hangover, the pigs as a group walking on their hind legs, and the sale of the timber to Frederick (whose role is very minor). Small details are altered; it is Boxer, not Snowball and Napoleon, who break into the farmhouse; Boxer's collapse is an accident because a wheel falls off the cart he is pulling, not the result of chronic exhaustion; Boxer is not attacked by the dogs; the horse slaughterer's van is mechanised, not drawn by horses; and the rewriting of the "all animals are equal" is not backed up by erasing all the others (see chapter 10). Chapters 7 and 8 of the book are very much shortened in this film version.

The film adds the use of listening equipment, which enables Pilkington to overhear the animals talking amongst themselves. It turns Squealer into a maker of propaganda films, and the executions of the "guilty" animals are staged in those films, not in front of the animals, which reduces their shock value. Squealer uses the distraction of television to divert the animals from the pigs' misdeeds. In the film, he is probably the most interesting character.

Most importantly, the film ends happily, with Napoleon dead, and a new human family owning the farm. The end of the film links to its (invented) prologue, where Jessie tells us that Napoleon's evil dream has been washed away by a storm because it was built on the wrong foundations. She and other animals went into hiding and simply waited for Napoleon to die.

The film does not try to give the same weight to ideological issues as Orwell. Old Major's speech is reduced to a few quotations, and "Beasts of England" has different words and little resonance. The characterisation of Pilkington reduces the focus on Napoleon's selfishness and greed, and the repressive violence- the reign of terror- does not come through in the film.

None of these points are necessarily criticisms. They simply prove the principle that films are adaptations, "based on" books. This one does not set out to translate Orwell's text faithfully on to the screen.

This means that you should be careful about using the film as the basis for your own essays or notes, because the differences are important.

Characters and their role in the story

Mr Jones

He used to be a capable farmer, but now he is usually drunk; he drinks beer, more than is good for him, probably because he has lost a lawsuit- no details are given. He keeps a shotgun in his bedroom. He was always a hard master but is disheartened and more cruel now. He reads the "News of the World" and sleeps during the day (when he should be looking after the farm and the animals on it). He has four farmhands. They are all hated by the animals. He uses a whip to control them, thrash and maltreat them. After the Rebellion, he sits in the Red Lion pub complaining about the injustice of the revolution. He attacks the farm in chapter 4, carrying a gun, and bringing all his men. He shoots at Snowball and wounds him. In chapter 6, he has given up hope of getting the farm back and has gone to live elsewhere. At the start of chapter 10, we are told that he has died in a shelter for alcoholics.

We can understand why Old Major thinks that the interests of farmers and their animals are incompatible, and that farmers have no interest in animal welfare, when farmers like Jones are free to oppress animals.

Old Major

He is the prize Middle White boar (called Willingdon Beauty); aged 12; rather stout; majestic-looking, wise and benevolent. He has had "over four hundred children". He has considerable rhetorical skill, and is a visionary. He dies three days after his speech, at the end of chapter 1.

His complaints about human cruelty seem not to apply so much to his own life, which has been relatively leisurely and comfortable. He is a boar, kept to breed generations of pigs, which are sold at the age of 1, for meat.

Napoleon

A young boar at the start of the narrative; he is a large, rather fierce-looking Berkshire, not much of a talker, but with a reputation for getting his own way. He has depth of character (we might call this determination).

From the moment of the rebellion- when the animals break into the food store- he controls all the food supplies, and makes all the decisions about rations; he releases food as a reward for bravery in battle, in chapter 8.

He is not interested in educating adult animals; only in indoctrinating the young. He is careful to organise support for himself, especially among the sheep. He produces no ideas of his own, but criticises Snowball's ideas and always opposes them, especially the windmill. He argues for a strong, armed defence of Animal Farm.

He sets his dogs on Snowball, and then decrees that decisions about the management of the farm will now be a private matter among the remaining pigs. At the end of chapter 6, he acts out a calculated charade, in which he blames Snowball (not his own faulty design) for the destruction of the almost finished windmill in the November storm. He repeats this performance, ominously, in chapter 7, preparing the ground for the public execution of several animals, as a way of intimidating the rest, four days later.

In chapter 7, he tricks Whymper into thinking there is no shortage of food on the farm. He now spends all his time in the farmhouse (guarded by dogs), and seldom speaks to the working animals. He puts down the hens' protest in chapter 7 by starving nine of them to death. He has awarded himself both of the military decorations- although he did not, himself, fight in the Battle of the Cowshed in chapter 4.

In chapter 8, he has reduced his public appearances to less than one a fortnight, and he has added a cockerel to his entourage of dogs, so that his speeches are always introduced by a fanfare. His paranoia, and his sense of self-importance, are growing. His birthday is celebrated publicly, with a gun salute, and he has a number of official titles- some are sinister, some ridiculous, but they all (invented by the pigs) reflect, and reinforce, the other animals' servility and his intimidation of them. In chapter 8, he has his food tasted by a pig called Pinkeye, in case anyone is trying to poison him. When he inspects the completed windmill, he announces that it will be named Napoleon Mill, after himself.

He makes the serious tactical mistake of alienating Pilkington and selling the timber to Frederick, who deceives him by paying for it with forged banknotes. There is a premature celebratory scene in the barn, where the animals have to file past Napoleon and admire him as he reclines majestically on a platform.

When this vanity is shown to be misplaced, and his stupidity in being deceived by Frederick is clear, there is more bad news for Napoleon- Frederick attacks the farm, heavily armed, and Pilkington refuses to help. The windmill is blown up- destroyed for a second time- because Napoleon's diplomacy has been misjudged. He himself suffers a chip in his tail from a pellet- which shows that he was, literally, fighting in the rear!

Two days of celebrations afterwards induce the animals to forget about the forged banknotes- their worthlessness has made it impossible to buy the machinery needed for the windmill. From Napoleon's point of view, its destruction saves him some potential embarrassment. He rewards himself with the new military honour, the Order of the Green Banner.

Napoleon has the worst hangover imaginable, after drinking whisky- it is so bad that his death seems to the other pigs to be imminent. In a rare, unselfish gesture- potentially the last one of his life- he decrees that drinking alcohol should be punishable by death (an ironic reference to Old Major's original instruction). Two days later, fully recovered, he decides that the farm must start to brew its own alcohol- for the benefit and use of the pigs only, of course. Once production starts, every pig is allowed one pint of beer each day, but Napoleon is entitled to four.

In chapter 9, thirty-one piglets are born, in four separate litters. These are Napoleon's children- a schoolroom will be built for them. Meanwhile, they are kept separate from other animals, and given privileges, to reinforce their sense of their own superiority, and the other animals' sense of their own inferiority.

Although he now weighs 24 stone, Napoleon eats sugar, but does not allow the other pigs any, because it will make them fat; a fine example of self-delusion.

In chapter 9, he is elected as President of the Republic of Animal Farm; he is, of course, the only candidate. At the end of the chapter, having organised Boxer's death, he makes a political and self-regarding speech, and tells the other animals that the pigs (he means, only the pigs) will have a memorial banquet for him. We know that the true meaning of this is that their taste for whisky is so strong that they will sell their most faithful labouring animal, to an executioner, to pay for more drink.

In chapter 10, the windmill is finished, but Napoleon still denies the animals electricity, on the (untrue) basis that the secret to happiness is not heat, light and comfort but hard work and a hard life of poverty. He parades, on two legs, holding a whip (like Jones); he starts smoking; he wears Jones' clothes, and his "favourite sow" wears one of Mrs Jones' smartest dresses. He tells Pilkington and the delegation of human farmers that there is nothing revolutionary about Animal Farm; that they do not wish to spread their ideology to other farms (nations); they are dropping the form of address "comrade", and any revolutionary rituals, including their old flag. They are even reverting to the old, "correct and original" name of The Manor Farm- thus pouring soil on the coffin of revolution. Discarding the title of Animal Farm is the same as discarding every revolutionary instinct, principle or belief.

Napoleon is a calculating, power-hungry pig. He exploits his fellow animals, and will murder as many of them as he needs to, in cold blood, in order to preserve his own position of power. He also thinks ahead- his legacy to his children will be a world in which they will be the master race, all-powerful and unchallenged.

Snowball

He is more vivacious than Napoleon, quicker in speech and more inventive. He weighs 15 stone. He breaks into the farmhouse when Jones has fled. He is the best of the animals at writing. He rewrites the name of the farm, as Animal Farm, on the five-bar gate. He paints the seven commandments on the barn wall. He designs the flag with the horn and the hoof on it, and explains its symbolism to the other animals.

He sets up (unsuccessful) Animal Committees, and successful reading and writing classes- almost all the animals can read and write to some extent. He simplifies the commandments into the slogan "four legs good, two legs bad". He opposes "human influences"; he is a revolutionary ideologue, a loyal disciple of Old Major's teachings.

He agrees that the pigs should have all the milk and apples. He designs the battle plans for the Battle of the Cowshed. He charges at Jones, who shoots him. He believes that "the only good human being is a dead one". He reminds the animals, after the Battle of the Cowshed, that they must be willing to die for the revolution if necessary.

He makes brilliant, persuasive speeches in debates. He is a great reader, and full of ideas to make the animals' lives easier. He finds the location for the windmill, which he says can supply electricity, so that the animals can have labour-saving technology; then he works out detailed plans in a shed he uses as a study. He argues that the best defence for the revolution is to provoke similar rebellions on other farms- this is the international socialism which Trotsky advocated.

After he is chased away, Snowball is blamed for everything that goes wrong- the destruction of the windmill at the end of chapter 6, and any accidental damage in chapter 7. Because of Napoleon's lies, he becomes, to the other animals, a menacing and dangerous, malignant, invisible threat, like an evil spirit.

His reputation is destroyed, by degrees, in spite of Boxer's protests. In chapter 9, it is aid that he was openly fighting on Jones' side, and leading it, in the Battle in chapter 4; nothing could be further from the truth.

Snowball is the leader the animals might have had, if they had been more intelligent. He could not have been worse than the one they had instead! Orwell was himself sympathetic to Trotsky, and critical of Stalin. This feeds into his characterisation of Snowball (Trotsky) and Napoleon (Stalin).

Squealer

He is a small fat pig with very round cheeks, twinkling eyes, nimble movements and a shrill voice, and a brilliant and persuasive talker, with a reputation for being able to "turn black into white". He takes over from Snowball as the re-educator of the animals, but, more accurately, he is the doer of Napoleon's mischief and dirty work.

He explains that the pigs need the milk and apples to feed their brains and keep Jones at bay. In chapter 5, he argues that, in banishing democracy and becoming an autocratic dictator, Napoleon is somehow sacrificing himself to the responsibility of leadership, in order to protect the animals from their own tendency to make bad decisions. At the end of chapter 5, he claims, outrageously, that the windmill was Napoleon's idea, and his opposition to it, when Snowball supported it, "tactical".

In chapter 6, he tells the animals that their vague sense that trading was always prohibited under the rules of Animalism must have been a dream or an illusion, because there are no written records of that idea.

He is needed again, to defend the pigs' inhabiting of the farmhouse; he says that they need a quiet place to work, and that Napoleon's dignity deserves something better than a sty to live in. He also argues- ludicrously- that there is a key distinction between blankets- which are allowed, under Animalism- and sheets, which, as a human invention, are not.

He delivers morale-boosting speeches on "the joy of service and the dignity of labour" (chapter 7). Then he tells the animals that Snowball is about to lead Frederick's attack on the farm, and that newly discovered secret documents (how convenient!) prove that Snowball was really Jones' secret agent.

His twinkling eyes become dangerous and sinister when he looks at Boxer in a "very ugly" way, and slaps down his reluctance to believe the latest anti-Snowball propaganda. Still in chapter 7, he reappears, to announce that the anthem "Beasts of England" has been banned, because the revolution is complete and there is no longer any need to sing about revolutionary sentiment.

In chapter 8, he has the task of reading out statistics which claim huge (made up) increases in productivity; the animals accept them unthinkingly, proving the old saying that if you say something often enough, people will believe it. He also makes tearful speeches in praise of Napoleon, and paints a public portrait of him, in white paint, in profile. Later in this same chapter, Squealer is still working to revise the history of the Battle of the Cowshed, claiming that Snowball was a coward, not its hero. Then he tries to claim that the Battle of the Windmill- a painful and costly rearguard action, in which Boxer has suffered wounds he will never wholly recover from- is a famous victory.

Hampered by a severe hangover himself, he announces that Napoleon is so desperately ill (from drinking too much whisky) that he is about to die. A few days later, he is sent out, in the middle of the night, to change the fifth commandment on the wall of the barn, regarding the consumption of alcohol. Being drunk, he falls off his ladder, but not until he has amended it, to permit drinking, except "to excess".

In chapter 9, he has to defend the reduction (or "re-adjustment") in rations which favours pigs and dogs and harms the other animals. His alleged "proofs" that there is more food for all the animals than there ever was under Jones are now desperately flawed, and the voice he announces them in- "a shrill rapid voice"- suggests that even he does not believe, and cannot justify, his own message. But still the animals believe everything he tells them, because they have lost their memories and their judgment, and they still want to cling to the belief that their lives now are better; otherwise, the revolution would have been a waste of time and effort.

His clinching argument is that the "freedom" they have achieved is better than their previous lives as slaves. Ironically, of course, Napoleon has taken way their freedom of speech and of thought, long ago.

In chapter 9, Spontaneous Demonstrations are introduced; Squealer has to read out meaningless and unreliable statistics there. When Boxer collapses, Squealer announces that Napoleon is sending him to an animal hospital for treatment; this, too, is an outrageous lie. He then has to announce, and explain, Boxer's death, which he turns into a propaganda piece, praising Napoleon. This story is so outrageous that even Squealer is not sure it will be believed.

In chapter 10, he spends a whole week coaching the sheep on a new slogan, so that when the pigs- including him- have mastered the art of walking on their hind legs, the sheep can salute their achievement with the fresh slogan, "Four legs good, two legs better!"

Minimus

This pig is not mentioned until at the end of chapter 5- he is described as a pig with a "remarkable gift" for composing songs and poems. This assessment of his skill is ironic, judging by the evidence of the second-rate poem "Comrade Napoleon" in chapter 8, and the small song at the end of chapter 7.

Pilkington

He is an easy-going gentleman-farmer who goes hunting or fishing most of the time. The animals distrust him. Pilkington has an important role (as Winston Churchill) in chapter 10, where he sets aside the mistrust of socialist states which is natural to the Western Allies, and tries to minimise the cultural differences which were to lead to the Cold War. There is a hint of appeasement in the subservient tone he adopts towards Napoleon; in 1943, the Allies needed Russia more than Russia, having repulsed Hitler, needed them. His argument that the interests of human farmers and pig farmers are the same- the highest possible productivity at the lowest possible cost- would be abhorrent to Old Major.

Frederick

Another farmer.He is tough and shrewd; he drives hard bargains; he is always involved in lawsuits. The animals fear and hate him, and there are widespread allegations of his extreme cruelty to animals (like Hitler's genocide against the Jews) in chapter 8.

Mr Whymper

He is a solicitor from Willingdon, who agrees to visit the farm every Monday (from chapter 6 onwards) and take orders from Napoleon; a sly-looking little man. He arranges the sale of 400 eggs per week (chapter 7); that figure goes up to 600, in chapter 9, to maintain the pigs' lifestyle. He advises Napoleon to sell the ten-year old pile of timber.

By chapter 10, he has been able to buy a dogcart of his own. This means he has made money out of his role on Animal Farm.

The dogs: Bluebell, Jessie and Pincher

At the start of this story, Old Major reminds the animals that Jones drowns his dogs when they can no longer work. They have all died (presumably, of natural causes) by the start of chapter 10.

They are relatively clever. The dogs, as a group, can read fairly well, but are only interested in reading the commandments.

Jessie and Bluebell produce nine puppies, which Napoleon keeps aside and turns into his private army, or secret police. They appear, suddenly, in chapter 5, where they are described as enormous/huge, though not yet fully grown, with snapping jaws; wearing brass-studded collars, as fierce as wolves, and utterly obedient to Napoleon.

It is because of the importance of his attack dogs that Napoleon exempts the dogs from the reductions in rations which apply to the other animals (chapter 9).

The cart-horses: Boxer and Clover

It was seeing a cart-horse being whipped by a boy that gave Orwell his first idea for an animal rebellion.

Boxer and Clover are the farm's two cart-horses. They are faithful disciples of animalism; unable to think for themselves; reliable followers, but not leaders. They are easily led and indoctrinated. **Boxer** burns his own straw hat on the fire, obeying Snowball. He has tremendous muscles and strength, and is a tireless worker- everyone admires him.

Boxer is an enormous beast, at nearly 18 hands high, and as strong as two ordinary horses. He looks somewhat stupid because of a white stripe down his nose and indeed is not of first-rate intelligence, but he is universally respected for his steadiness of character and tremendous powers of work.

He takes on extra work, starting half an hour earlier than the other animals. In chapter 6, he increases this daily voluntary work to 45 minutes; then, again, to an hour, in chapter 7. In order to complete the windmill, he works on his own for an hour or two, at night.

He is not very literate. He only knows the letters A,B,C and; he cannot remember more than four letters at a time. He kicks a stable-boy unconscious in the battle in chapter 4; but he does not mean to hurt or kill him.

In chapter 7, he manages to put into words his difficulty in accepting the propaganda which accuses Snowball of treason. Even though he backs down when Squealer contradicts him, Boxer's innocent sense of morality has now marked him out as an enemy of the regime- it is effectively his own death warrant. Napoleon's dogs try to attack him, but he is too strong.

Boxer challenges Squealer again, late in chapter 8, over his claim that the Battle of the Windmill is a great victory. He senses, too, that, at the age of 11, rebuilding the windmill again is now too big a task for him. Although he is injured, he refuses to work less hard than before; he ignores Clover's warning that he is risking his health.

In chapter 9, Napoleon invents the "Spontaneous Demonstration", in which Boxer and Clover are expected to carry a green banner inscribed with the words "Long live comrade Napoleon".

When Boxer collapses, he still hopes to live in retirement for three years, when he hopes he will learn the alphabet. Napoleon has other plans for him. So Boxer dies, a suspicious three days after being taken from the farm- to hospital, if Squealer is to be believed. We- and the other animals- know that Boxer has been sold to the knacker for money the pigs will spend on whisky.

Boxer has two personal mottos; "I will work harder", and, later, from chapter 5 onwards, "Napoleon is always right".

In a 1944 essay, Orwell criticised those who were in favour of allowing the Russians to be particularly severe on Germany, in setting out the post-war settlement (political and financial). He argued that you must be able to criticise another country if you want to co-operate with them properly, and that Britain and Russia cannot be true friends if our attitude is that "Stalin is always right". Boxer is wrong in trying to convince others, or himself, that Napoleon "is always right".

Clover, the other cart-horse, is a stout motherly mare approaching middle life; she has had four foals, which were sold at the age of one year old. She protects the ducklings which have lost their mother in the opening chapter.

She learns the alphabet but cannot read words or phrases. She seems able to say very little, but Orwell writes out her reaction to the vicious killing of animals in chapter 7, at length. Her thoughts and feelings here make her into a patient, longsuffering "mother Russia" type of figure, as she regrets what has gone so badly wrong on the farm, not just on her own account, but as a spokesman for the animals as a group.

She tries to look after Boxer's health in chapter 9, but he will not listen to her- with fatal results, for him. Although his wounds heal, his general appearance is becoming less healthy, as he gets older, but he still maintains his workload. Although he is now almost 12- only a month away from retirement age- he will not consider the need to ease off in his effort at a hugely physical job, dragging stone. It comes as no surprise to the reader when he falls down with a collapsed lung. Clover tries to warn him to break out of the van taking him to his death, but he cannot- he is too weak.

Clover is aged 14 at the end of the story- she still has not retired. There are three other horses, who work hard and are "very stupid"- even more stupid than the stupidly loyal Boxer had been; otherwise, they would not tolerate the way Napoleon (or, if not him, men) exploit them and their strength. She is going blind, and, now that Muriel is dead, she turns to Benjamin to read her the latest version of the commandments; and he delivers the revelation that they have been condensed into the single, final, insult, that some animals - namely the pigs - are "more equal than others".

She leads the group of taller animals who peer in at the farmhouse window with "wondering faces". She sees Pilkington treating the pigs as equals, and she watches, as cordial speeches are made, by him and Napoleon. To her "old dim eyes", the pigs and the humans are now the same. .

Muriel

She is a white goat. She can read well- she reads scraps of newspapers to the other animals.

In chapter 6, Clover relies on her to read out the "revised" fourth commandment, about sleeping in beds with sheets. Clover asks her to read out the latest version of the sixth commandment, at the start of chapter 8. It is through Muriel, again, that we learn what has been done to the fifth commandment, at the end of chapter 8. She has died by the time chapter 10 starts.

Benjamin

He is the donkey- the oldest animal on the farm, and the worst tempered. He seldom talks; he is usually cynical, and the only animal who never laughs. He is devoted to Boxer. His style is slow and obstinate; he does the work expected of him, and no more. He expresses no opinion about the Rebellion and its results. He can read anything. He is neutral about the windmill, doubting that life will become any easier because of it, or any other new invention.

Orwell once wrote about the mindset of "semi-anaesthesia" in which ordinary British civilians had lived through the bombing of London (in 1940). He concluded that, if you are in the midst of all sorts of horrors which you cannot change or prevent, this type of detachment is a way of coping. Benjamin is cynical about, or indifferent to, political movements and regimes, in the same way. He believes that, when you take the long view, nothing much changes. The failure of animalism to improve the animals' lives permanently justifies this point of view, eventually.

Benjamin knows that Boxer is being sent to his death in chapter 9; he reads out the wording on the van.

He is the only animal with a reliable memory. His experience tells him that, for animals, whoever is in charge, life always remains much the same- a mixture of hunger, hardship and disappointment.

Significantly, he says that those things are "the unalterable law of life". This is exactly the phrase Snowball and Napoleon had used to describe the commandments of Animalism in chapter 2. Benjamin's long experience means that, to him, the ideals which lie behind the Rebellion were always doomed to fail.

Mollie

This foolish, pretty, flirtatious white mare, who formerly drew Mr Jones' trap, minces daintily; wears ribbons; and likes sugar lumps.

She asks stupid questions; for example, will there be sugar after the Rebellion?

She is unconvinced of the need to rebel.

She admires herself in Mrs Jones' bedroom mirror, narcissistically. She shirks work, claiming to have a stone in her hoof; she sleeps in late. She is interested only in spelling out her own name (rather like a toddler).

She hides during the battle in chapter 4, and becomes work-shy in chapter 5.

Clover has seen her talking to one of Pilkington's men, who is in the process of luring her away with sugar and ribbons; three days later she disappears from the farm, and is seen several weeks later pulling a cart, dressed up and "enjoying herself". The animals never mention her again, after this.

Mollie symbolises a group of people who are always so caught up in their preoccupations with their image of themselves that they have no interest in what is going on in the society they live in. They are so apolitical that they take no notice of the revolution in their country/town/street. You may be surprised at how many of these people there are in your own community.

The cat

The cat does not listen to Major's speech. It votes both that (wild) rats are enemies, and that they are comrades; it never works, but appears at meal-times; and manages to stay away from the executions in chapter 7. Cats the world over are independent, resourceful, and detached; and so is Orwell's.

Moses

He is the tame raven, and Jones' pet. The other animals perceive him as a clever talker and a spy. He is hated for doing no work.

He spins a vision of heaven (Sugarcandy Mountain). Jones feeds him on bread crusts soaked in beer.

He reappears on the farm in chapter 9, after several years away. This is a clear sign that the animals' plight is now as bad as it was when Jones ran the farm. The pigs give him a gill of beer a day, which is a quarter of a pint; more than enough for a raven, you would think, and certainly a sign that they want to use him to distract the animals from the wretched state of their lives (just like the times before the Rebellion), when he was equally useful to Jones.

The other pigs

In chapter 1, the pigs without names are no different from the other animals, although they go to the front of the platform to hear Old Major's speech- perhaps because they are his children.

Pigs are generally recognised as the cleverest of the animals in this story. They teach themselves to read and write perfectly, so it is natural for them to lead, teach and organise the other animals.

They manage to milk the cows. They can think of a solution to every problem with harvesting, using tools designed for human use. They do not work on the harvest, but direct and supervise.

They are the only animals who put forward resolutions at the Sunday meetings. They use the harness-room as their headquarters, where they study farming skills from books in the evenings. By chapter 5, it is accepted that they should set farm policy out, and plan all the work.

In chapter 6, they start living in the farmhouse, and it is announced that they are to be allowed to sleep for an extra hour in the mornings.

They invent the string of flattering titles, which Napoleon allows to be attached to mentions of his name, in chapter 8. At the end of that chapter, they discover Jones' whisky; but they only discover the consequences of drinking it when they all have severe hangovers the next day. This is comically appropriate to pigs, which, by definition, lack restraint.

In chapter 10, the pigs have become a white-collar bureaucracy. The produce all manner of documents- and then, to prove their pointlessness, they burn them, rather than filing them. Half a dozen of the most eminent pigs mix comfortably with half a dozen of the human farmers in the final scene.

The pigs become the ruling animal class by virtue of their intellectual superiority. Orwell shows us that some animals are not bright enough to be leaders, but that pigs are too selfish and greedy to govern in accordance with principles of equality. Their innate greed will always get the better of them.

The pigs also display a range of points of view. Unlike other animals on the farm, they can both think and express their thoughts. The clearest example of this is when four young pigs object to Napoleon's abolition of democratic meetings in chapter 5, and to his decision- in chapter 6- to start trading with humans. Both times, the growling dogs silence them. These pigs are the first animals to be executed in the show trials in chapter 7. Napoleon's willingness to murder animals of his own kind – they must be relatives of his – proves that he is utterly ruthless in his appetite for power.

Hens

The hens resist the demand to surrender their eggs on the grounds that this is "murder". Napoleon starves them into submission; nine of them die (chapter 7). The three ringleaders are executed in chapter 7. Three more are put to death in chapter 8- after confessing that they were plotting to murder Napoleon!

Sheep

They mindlessly bleat "four legs good, two legs bad" for hours at a time. One sheep dies in the Battle of the Cowshed in chapter 4. They bleat their slogan in meetings, and during Snowball's speeches; Napoleon has trained them to be loyal to him. They break into this slogan-bleating at difficult moments, such as right at the end of chapter 7.

They particularly like the Spontaneous Demonstrations (chapter 9) where they can do a lot of meaningless bleating.

In chapter 10, although it takes a week, they are re-educated, by Squealer, in a new slogan- "four legs good, two legs better"- to endorse the pigs' final moves towards aping human beings.

Power and its uses- a key theme

Old Major and Napoleon are both boars - deeply English animals - on a farm in England. Major has been allowed to live on into old age, as he is needed on the farm, to breed pigs, but all the other animals are killed for food, or sold, at a young age. Man has power over the life and death of these powerless animals, and, while they live, he exploits their labour, taking the eggs and milk they produce and the crops they have helped to cultivate. Old Major is wise, and unselfish. He incites the animals to rebel, at the end of his own life, so that their lives can be better.

Napoleon and Snowball are young boars- they do not have Old Major's experience. They are clever; Napoleon is greedy, ruthless, and motivated by the desire to wield power- megalomania. Any concern he has to make the animals' lives better soon evaporates. While he is, clearly, a representation of Stalin, against Snowball's Trotsky, he is, more broadly, symbolic of dictators everywhere- of his namesake, Napoleon Bonaparte, of Hitler, Mao Tse-tung in China, and, perhaps, Franco in Spain.

Stalin's purges, the suffering of the kulaks, and the hardships of the modernising of the Russian economy find their symbols in the executions of the animals at the show trials in chapter 7, and of Boxer; in the starving of the hens; and in the windmill. Napoleon is like Stalin; his monstrous elimination of dissent enables him to corrupt and kill off the social progress which the rebellion had achieved. He is cynical and without conscience in the way he exploits the idealism, aspiration and goodwill with which the animals had become willing agents of a rebellion which he perverts for his own personal benefit.

The dictator uses the power of the spoken and written word to reinforce his own control. Squealer's relentless and energetic stream of pronouncements changes the animals' perception of events in the past- even the recent past. Snowball was a hero, not a traitor; but Napoleon derives authority from turning him into an enemy of the people.

Moses the raven symbolises the power of religious belief, which is anti-revolutionary. Typically religion tells us to endure our suffering in life for a reward after we are dead. Thus religion flourishes where there is oppression.

Moses is Jones' pet. When the rebellion energises the animals to improve their own lives, here and now, he disappears. He only returns, in chapter 9, at the point when the animals' distress becomes as acute as it had been in the last days of Jones' regime. In other words, he returns when they 'need' religion.

Orwell wrote that the idea of using farm animals in his story came to him when he saw a small boy, of perhaps ten, whipping and driving a huge cart-horse. The animals have a latent power which they fail to use; perhaps they are not intelligent enough to realise what they are capable of.

Orwell observed that the critical moment in the story is at the end of Chapter 2; the animals fail to challenge Napoleon over what will be done with the five buckets of milk. That lack of assertiveness shows Napoleon that he can realise his ambition of exercising absolute authority over the animals, because they are too weak to resist.

Boxer is physically powerful enough to kill the vicious dogs, but he is misguided in his misplaced loyalty to Napoleon.

Napoleon and Snowball can read and write. They formulate the seven commandments. Napoleon uses Squealer to modify them, and, finally, to wipe them out. He uses Squealer's facility with words to build up his own cult, and to compensate for his own lack of eloquence. Squealer's function as the deliverer of Napoleon's orders gives Napoleon more time and space to embed the supremacy of the pigs (he fathers 31); to create a social hierarchy, with the pigs, then the dogs, at the apex of it; to live a life of luxury and become 24 stones in weight; and to calculate a strategy to make the farm (Russia) accepted by its neighbours (internationally, Britain and the West). Maintaining his own power means that Napoleon will deprive the working animals of any power over their own livelihoods they had gained for themselves.

Ominously, where Jones had no children, Napoleon has bred a large clan of pigs, who will, presumably, maintain the class system they are born into. They will be educated in the school room the other animals have built; will eat the food the other animals have produced; and will be, as Jones was, "the lord of all the animals". A bleak future beckons; the animals will not rebel against their own kind, and, if they try to, the pigs will have the means to destroy them in a civil war.

Orwell wanted to write a tale to show that the cycle of rebellion for the good of the many is inevitably followed by the consolidation of power by the few, for their own selfish ends. Napoleon's selfish drives become clearer and clearer. Finally, he is as uninterested in revolution as Mollie was.

The aims of the revolution are forgotten, or deliberately erased from history and the general consciousness; any gains it brought are thrown away. Orwell dramatizes the principle, by showing us the progressive betrayal of the seven commandments, until there is, finally, nothing to differentiate these pigs (the socialists) from these farmers (the capitalist nations).

We should note that, while Napoleon grabs power eagerly, the animals are complicit too. They make it easy for him. They have too little education and ambition. They are like Benjamin the donkey who refuses to be involved in the political process. Orwell believed that a society like England's would always be safe from totalitarianism because public opinion makes itself heard; while we abhor violent protest, and are good at not killing one another, we know that our governments will be reined in by our capacity to disapprove of them. The animals do not express themselves, and Squealer is quick to stamp on any signs of dissent. The conditions for totalitarian dictatorship depend partly on the sort of inert, passive, poorly educated proletariat which the working animals make up.

Writing techniques and how they control the narrative

Orwell is adept at controlling his narrative. Intense, close-up scenes are interspersed with a wider view of the landscape of the farm. There are moments of hope, or even joy, and moments of grief and helplessness.

The narrative voice is journalistic and neutral. It presents events without overt judgment (Orwell uses language to steer us towards a correct interpretation of events), rather like a documentary or reality television programme. But the reader is always clear about how to interpret each piece of behaviour and each episode

Orwell uses irony, foreshadowing, comedy, and dramatic tension to animate his narrative. You should be able to find many examples; I encourage you to go through the text, looking for them, because this is the best way to analyse Orwell's narrative method. Here are a few, to point you in that direction.

Irony

The sheep follow Napoleon slavishly. They are in the habit of bleating "four legs good, two legs bad", because Snowball had to summarise the commandments for them in this simplistic form, so that they can remember them. In chapter 10, Squealer takes the sheep aside for a whole week, on to some waste ground at the far end of the farm, to indoctrinate them with a new slogan which seeks to make the pigs' shocking decision to walk on their hind legs respectable. The phrase is: "four legs good, two legs better". The irony is both comic- because the sheep are so unintelligent, it takes so long- and dramatic, because the new slogan drives home this final betrayal of the values of Animalism with particular emotional force for the reader.

Foreshadowing

Old Major addresses Boxer directly in his speech and reminds him that when he has no strength left Jones will send him to the knacker's. This prophecy or prediction comes true; it is just that Napoleon, not Jones, is the architect of it. Boxer's mild resistance to Squealer's denigrating of Snowball's courage is harmless. But, in the paranoid world of the dictator, it is disloyal enough to make him an "enemy of the state".

Comedy

The pigs' experiments drinking whisky in chapter 8 lead to the mother of all hangovers. Squealer falls off his ladder, and Napoleon is so ill that he is thought to be dying; his drunken antics, running round the farmyard, are manic. The comedy turns sour when the pigs annexe the retirement field for growing barley, which they will use to brew beer for themselves, and when Napoleon is so desperate for more whisky that he sells Boxer's life to buy it.

Dramatic tension

There is less drama in the battle scenes than we might expect; but they are not real battles, with graphic close-up images of wounding and slaughter. Orwell reserves that for the show trial and executions in chapter 7—a scene so shocking that neither of the two film versions includes it on camera.

In just four paragraphs, Orwell creates an ominous atmosphere, which the animals sense. The violence has tremendous force because it is described so matter-of-factly ("the dogs promptly tore their throats out"), and because a series of animals comes forward to be killed, even after they have seen what has been done to the first few. Their bravery in doing this is not explained- who would voluntarily step forward, to be ripped apart by wolf-like dogs in public? This missing element enables us, as readers, to feel the same kind of terror, in a milder form, for ourselves.

Look at Boxer's departure from the farm in chapter 9. The knacker's van is motorised in the film versions, but Orwell makes it drawn by horses (so that horses are betraying one of their own kind, not knowing that they are taking him to his death). He highlights the animals' helplessness, because they know that they cannot rescue Boxer and he cannot escape. We share their horror as they realise the truth about what type of vehicle it is, and where it is taking Boxer.

Symmetry

The process of Orwell's narrative is attractively simple (like a fairy tale). He shows us how the rebellion comes about, and the principles which motivate it. Then he shows us, in the subsequent chapters, how those principles are destroyed, by the pigs' cynicism and greed and the other animals' lack of intelligence. Having the seven commandments (and, in addition, the smaller points which Old Major included in his speech as warnings- no smoking, no touching money, no trading) gives a neat structure- it is like a building, which is slowly but systematically dismantled and demolished. This is the house the pigs built!

Napoleon takes over from Old Major as the pre-eminent boar; like Old Major, he has many "children", but a very different vision of how the world should be. Old Major lacked the power to see his vision turned into reality, but it was designed to abolish misery. Napoleon has the power to realise his own vision, which is selfish, and needlessly cruel to the other animals. Their lives, after the revolution, are worse than ever, and there is no prospect of improving them, because Napoleon has made sure that a dynasty of pigs will continue to rule the other animals, as a Fascist master race.

Napoleon's propaganda and methods of terrorising them have damaged, or wiped away, the animals' thoughts, memories, and freedoms. Squealer has a vital role, in influencing them to be obedient. He uses the threat of violence to achieve this- he is accompanied by the vicious dogs.

It is interesting to note that, while Old Major **says** he had a dream, and therefore attaches a supernatural or mystical force to his vision, as well as setting it to music ("Beasts of England"), this, too, could just be his own invention- a piece of propaganda.

We can see Orwell's fable as an illustration of the law of unintended consequences. The animals trust in Napoleon, but he kills Boxer, just as Jones would have done. Jones killed his pigs for ham; Napoleon kills a variety of animals, to terrorise them into submission (or "loyalty").

As we read the story, we track two things- the revision of the seven commandments, until nothing is left of them, and the parallel destruction of truth, history and Snowball's reputation. We know that the telling of the tale will be complete when none of the commandments remains to be broken.

The seven commandments of animalism, like the ten commandments of the Old Testament, are designed as a way of organising society, so that everyone can live harmoniously, with selfish personal drives being kept in check. Old Major is rather like an Old Testament prophet; Napoleon is like the naughty child who turns into a bully, and believes that rules are there to be broken. Dictators construct their own rules, and force their subjects to follow them.

The 1999 film version replaces a bad human farmer with a good one, at its end. But this contradicts what Orwell wanted the message of his story to be. In his own telling of Animal Farm, Orwell replaces a large, old, principled boar with another one, whose intentions are only to perpetuate his own power and comfort. It is a bleak ending.

Essays and how to write them

Essay technique is a vital part of your armoury when you're fighting for good grades in your exams. It's easy to learn, and to put into practice. It's also very easy to underperform, and do yourself less than justice, by ignoring it.

If you were a professional sportsman or woman, or a professional musician, and your living depended on your results, you would make sure you practise your skills, every day, so that they are sharp and familiar, and you can rely on them under pressure.

Essay writing needs to become a skill in exactly the same way- because your future income and prospects may be affected by your exam grades.

Really.

The exam questions we're dealing with require you to-

-understand the question

-plan and organise your answer

-write clearly and correctly

The various exam boards' reports find the same mark-losing and grade-losing mistakes year after year. Please don't fall into these well-signposted traps- NOT answering the question; NOT planning your answer, or overplanning it; NOT sticking to the question; NOT using your time properly.

Under the pressure of a real exam, many people just panic. They don't read the question closely enough, or they misread it, or they answer the question they wish had been set, or they start writing in the quotations they've learnt, whether they are relevant or not.

At least as many candidates then decide not to make a plan- even though the exam paper will probably point out that planning time is included in the time you're given.

The answer booklet is full of blank pages. For some people, the challenge seems to be to fill in all of those pages- with quantity, not quality.

If you stick to the question, follow through and develop each of your points, from your plan, and write a short conclusion, then less is more!

What happens if you don't plan?

Your essay will wander off the subject of the question. You won't know when you've finished your answer, so you may be tempted to write some more….and some more….and some more…and run out of time for your other question, and throw away handfuls of marks as a result. Just through being disorganised.

You can avoid this! You simply need to practise beforehand, and stay focused in the exam itself.

So, let's look at your essay plan.

It will be brief, in the form of a spidergram with phrases of no more than two or three words. It will gather together all the material you will be using to answer the question. Don't write your point out fully until you're writing your answer. When you write the essay, you will write out the points and phrases in your plan, expanding them into explained sentences and paragraphs.

You must use your material in a way which shows why it is relevant and what it brings to your overarching argument. Short references and quotations will help here. Do not fill your answer with quotations! Time spent writing out long quotations is like time you spend narrating the story of the book- it means there's not enough analysis, and too little evidence that you have a view or response of your own.

Your plan will need to have perhaps seven or eight points in it.

Your opening should not be of the uncertain "I am going to write about…." variety. That sounds like a tired old car engine struggling to start on a cold winter morning.

Make your opening sentence or two a clear statement of your point of view. This will keep you on track.

Then prioritise your points, and use the most important ones first. Why? Because, if you run out of time, you will have made your most important points, which will be the most interesting ones for the marker of your essay to read.

Now, we're going to apply this method and use it to create answers to two essay questions. See whether you agree with me that this is a guaranteed way to get the most out of your ideas, and manage your time in the exam in order to maximise your marks.

Sample Essay 1

"Animal Farm" is a warning that power corrupts all who have it; the only workable society is one where everyone is equal. To what extent do you agree?

Plan

Napoleon, pigs, humans all corrupted by power. Equal sounds good; but animals are more intelligent or more stupid. Easily led means easily exploited and mistreated. Propaganda corrupts society. Napoleon sidelines democracy and terrorises farm (allegory/1917). Animals resist Jones but fail to resist Napoleon. Allow commandments to be rewritten. When should they have protested? No freedom of speech or thought. Defeat of animalism- avoidable? Snowball better?

Answer

Both Napoleon and the pigs with whom he forms a new bourgeoisie are so corrupt by the end of Orwell's "fairy tale" that they can no longer be distinguished from human beings. Old Major had insisted that the cause of the animals' oppression, slavery and cruel premature slaughter was Man, and his vision was of a world where all animals were equal because decisions were made by them, and for the benefit of all of them. By owning the farm co-operatively, and by providing for the needs of all animals, both working and retired, the animals, after the Rebellion, would have better lives because equality was embedded in the commandments of Animalism.

Orwell presents the problem that the theory here and the practical experience are rather different. The pigs become the intelligentsia, and do the brainwork, because the other animals are less able to think for themselves; they have poor memories and they cannot express their thoughts properly. Boxer and Clover are not very bright, even though they are cleverer than the sheep. Boxer's natural loyalty, and his naïve belief that the answer to any problem is "I will work harder" and "Napoleon is always right", allows Squealer to intimidate him, and control him with strong propaganda messages. Boxer's lack of intellectual power means that he has no social power, and no chance of escaping the gruesome death which the cruel and unsentimental Napoleon organises (and which Old Major had predicted, but under a human, not an animal regime).

Napoleon has singled Boxer out as a potential troublemaker because he will not accept without question the lies about Snowball's treachery. Therefore Napoleon plans to dispose of him, even though Boxer's contribution is so important to the work on the farm. "Loyalty" (or mindless obedience) is the only way of staying alive, once Napoleon is in charge.

After the key moment when Napoleon seizes absolute power in chapter 5, he justifies it, sending Squealer to argue that the animals themselves "might make the wrong decisions"- such as choosing Snowball as their leader. Orwell is interested in the failure of Napoleon to remain a democrat, and in the failure of the USSR to maintain the aims of the Russian Revolution of 1917 because of Stalin's repressive and totalitarian approach to the use of the power to govern. He is also interested in the theory of the "social contract", which the 17th century English political scientist Thomas Hobbes had argued was the best form of government; a benevolent dictatorship.

Orwell drew readers' attention to the moment at the end of chapter 3 where Napoleon takes the milk. The fact that the animals do not insist on distributing it allows the pigs to take all the apples, too, then the whisky, the barley, more of the food, and, eventually, to become the parasite which exploits and depends on the animals' labour- just like Jones.

Napoleon's intentions are not altogether clear, because Orwell is less interested in him than in the effects of his behaviour on the other animals. His resemblance to Stalin (cult of personality, use of propaganda to rewrite history, show trials, exile of Snowball/Trotsky, use of starvation to end the hens' revolt) is thorough, but we do not know at what point dictators (Napoleon Bonaparte and Hitler too) start to care only about maintaining their power. If the animals had resisted Napoleon's early tests of autocracy, the progressive betrayal and revision of the commandments, until only the one reinforcing the pigs' elite status, would not have taken place.

Their lack of intelligence combines with a lack of scepticism and the passivity we have just examined, to give Napoleon control. The animals are made to march round the perimeter in "spontaneous demonstrations", flanked by the dogs, and they dare not talk in front of the pigs or dogs.

After the rebellion the animals had explored the boundary fences of the farm with elation, but Napoleon drives them to despair through hunger and overwork. Napoleon dismantles democracy, by abolishing voting, then abolishing discussion at meetings; decisions are made by pigs only, and in their own interests.

When Napoleon is deceived by Frederick, with the forged banknotes, the "unfortunate" event is soon forgotten, in the lengthy, staged celebrations after the Battle of the Windmill. Squealer insists that holding on to what they had before is a victory; Boxer senses the essential lack of truth in all Squealer says, but neither he nor Clover have the clarity of memory to contradict him; and the killing of animals from time to time (the gander, well after the show trials) reminds the rest that dissent will not be tolerated.

Even as the audience files into the barn to hear Old Major's speech, there is an unofficial hierarchy among the animals; equality is an abstract concept which needs more than a vague commitment to democracy to make it real. The animals are too easily led (and not just the sheep).

Orwell's point is that, for totalitarian and repressive regimes to endure, two factors have to work together- the lack of intelligent resistance or questioning, and an individual with a ruthless character. He believed that the English people would never consent to a dictatorship because we are reluctant to kill each other, and tolerant of different convictions and ideologies; our statistics can generally be relied upon, and we would not accept the fictions about productivity which Stalin fed to the Russian people, and Squealer feeds to the animals.

Snowball's bid for power was rooted in the desire to improve the animals' lives. His model of Animalism might have been truer to Old Major's ideals, to begin with; but Snowball did not anticipate a power struggle. He was naïve, and naivete is not a quality that leaders, or nations, can afford to have. It is both sad and ironic that Napoleon tears up the last remnants of Animalism, and that he looks the same as Jones, in Jones' clothes. He created a power vacuum, by exiling Snowball. Once he had filled it, the animals needed to find ways of keeping him in check. The crimes are his, but the responsibility, as well as the consequent suffering, are theirs.

Power corrupts Napoleon, but the animals are not clever enough to govern themselves. Orwell acknowledges that someone has to be in charge. He is warning us to choose that person with care, and to keep them in check.

1065 words

Sample Essay 2

How does Orwell make Snowball such an important figure in the story as a whole?

Plan

Before and after exile. Idealistic, outward-looking. Trotsky v Stalin. His mistakes- lack of support/ pigs and apples. Later- contrast with Napoleon. Made into scapegoat, enemy of the state. Not there to defend self/ others don't defend. Progressive rewriting history and rewriting commandments. Victims on farm and off farm.

Answer

Snowball is important as a potential leader and improver of society on the farm. He is even more important once Napoleon's dogs have driven him away in chapter 5. He becomes a symbol of the power of propaganda, as his courage at the Battle of the Cowshed is revised, to cowardice, then to treason, for which Napoleon sentences him to death.

The windmill is Snowball's idea. Being able to generate electricity will give the animals an easier life, and a three-day working week. A better life was the aim of the (Bolshevik) uprising, and Snowball wants to send the pigeons to promote international socialism. He is an idealist; he capers around his plans for the windmill because he is excited at the thought of improving life for every animal.

He underestimates the attraction of power to the unprincipled and vicious Napoleon. He is wrong to defend the idea that the pigs need the apples (this is his pig-like greed coming to the fore). He fails to build strong enough support for his ideas among the animals; he is too wrapped up in his plans to notice what Napoleon is doing with the dogs. His banishment raises in the reader's mind what qualities the leader of a nation needs. Snowball does not have a well enough developed sense of danger.

The Battle of the Cowshed in chapter 4 gives the facts; Snowball led and won it. The animals cannot remember what the reader can. Boxer senses that Squealer is lying when he defames Snowball, but he does not have the power the reader has to resist or reject those lies. The animals' inability to argue back against propaganda- just like the seizure of the apples- enables Napoleon to do as he likes and disregard the animals, who become economic slaves, without the power to vote. Napoleon uses a lack of rations for them, and a culture of overwork, to drive out any resistance- hence the return of Moses and the comfort of Sugarcandy Mountain in chapter 9.

Snowball serves Orwell well, in allowing him to make the point that dictators remove inconvenient people from the official history, and that propaganda can turn white into black. The lies told about Snowball help us to judge Napoleon's regime as evil; it is morally corrupt as well as exploitative, because it has no time for truth or integrity. It is no surprise that the animals who do not defend Snowball's reputation cannot defend Boxer when Napoleon decides to have him killed (this ironically aligns Napoleon with Jones, who, Old Major had predicted, would send Boxer to the Knacker's). Snowball cannot defend himself because he is not there; and we cannot defend Animalism because we are only readers- we are at a distance from the farm too.

Hand in hand with the escalating defamation of Snowball goes the breaking of the seven commandments and the increasingly outrageous behaviour of the pigs (milk and apples; beds; alcohol; ribbons in tails, education, extra sleep, exemption from hard labour, management jobs, clothes, walking on hind legs, social superiority, priority over oncoming animals on the paths, parties). The blackening of Snowball's reputation mirrors the cynical and darkening atmosphere on the farm, until it is renamed "The Manor Farm". The threat of Snowball (in league with the farm's human enemies) is like the threat that Jones will come back; by creating a bogeyman, Napoleon diverts criticism and attention from his own failures and his cruelty, selfishness and obsession with power.

Urinating on the plans for the windmill, then claiming they were his, and using the gains from the windmill for the benefit of the pigs, not the whole community, are actions typical of Napoleon, who is deeply anti-social.

It is the role of Snowball to be a victim of Napoleon's greed for power, both on the farm and away from it; he becomes a symbol of the consuming and destructive power of propaganda. A hero, he is turned into a villain. Having taken up the mission of Old Major, he becomes a victim of Napoleon (though he escapes with his life) and the opposition who is suppressed and eliminated. When Snowball escapes the dogs through a hole in the hedge, all hope disappears with him; the rebellion turns to a reign of terror from which there is no escape, because a new generation of pigs is ready to take on Napoleon's repressive regime in succession to him.

760 words

Final tips for success

You'll have seen in the example essays that what counts is organising what you want to say (your plan), then working steadily and concisely through it. You have also seen that it is not the quantity of the words but their appropriateness that counts – essay two is more than 300 words shorter, yet packs the same punch.

What would be even better? Knowing what question you will be given! That is impossible.....but you can be sure that the questions you are given will be fair, and are designed to let you show how well you understand the set text, and the quality of your response to it. The examiner is not trying to 'catch you out' – the examiner is trying to 'mark you in'.

Whatever your exam board is, look on its website, not just at questions on past papers. Pay attention to the mark schemes and the comments in the examiners' reports. Ask your English teacher to go through the marking criteria; make sure that you know how to get the best possible mark.

…And a pitfall to avoid

Don't fall into the trap of having a list of quotations you're determined to force into any essay. If you know the book- which, surely, you must, by now!- suitable short references will pop into your mind.

Your number one focus is on answering the question in front of you.

Your number two focus is on answering the question.

So is focus number three.

We could go on!

Answering the question means taking it apart and highlighting the key words (often, that little word "how"); making a proper plan, which organises your material, gives you an argument and leads you to a clear and convincing conclusion; writing your essay from the plan; and stopping when you get to the end.

A proper plan leads to an essay that needs nothing added after its conclusion, because all your points are in your plan.

Don't think "I'll just write another paragraph or two", because that will lose you focus, structure, marks and time.

Please, please resist the temptation to start writing your answer straight away, even if many others in the exam room do precisely that. The exam builds in planning time. Use it to plan.

Finally, keep your focus on what the question requires you to do. Check- constantly- that what you are writing is answering the question you have chosen. If it isn't, leave it out.

Especially if you are taking your GCSE this coming summer, I wish you every success.

Gavin Smithers is a private tutor, covering Broadway, Chipping Campden, the North Cotswolds and Evesham. He has an English degree from Oxford University, and a passion for helping you to discover the joy and satisfaction of understanding great literature.

Gavin's Guides are short books packed with insight. Their key aim is to help you raise your grade!

The series is available in paperback and e-book formats. Details and reviews of the series are on Gavin Smithers' Amazon page.

Titles include:

> *Understanding J.B. Priestley's An Inspector Calls*
> *Understanding William Golding's Lord of the Flies*
> *Understanding Charles Dickens' Great Expectations*
> *Understanding John Steinbeck's Of Mice and Men*
> *Understanding Emily Dickinson's Set Poems*
> *Understanding Edward Thomas' Set Poems*

Understanding Andrew Marvell's Cromwell & Eulogy Poems
Understanding Harper Lee's To Kill A Mockingbird

And finally………..if there's anything you're still not sure about, and if your teacher can't help you, please contact the author-
grnsmithers@hotmail.co.uk

8299592R00068

Printed in Germany
by Amazon Distribution
GmbH, Leipzig